BET THE HOUSE

How I Gambled Over a Grand a Day for 30 Days on Sports, Poker, and Games of Chance

RICHARD ROEPER

CHICAGO
REVIEW
PRESS

Library of Congress Cataloging-in-Publication Data

Roeper, Richard, 1959–

    Bet the house : how I gambled over a grand a day for 30 days on sports, poker, and games of chance / Richard Roeper. — 1st ed.

       p. cm.

    Includes index.

    ISBN 978-1-56976-247-9

    1. Roeper, Richard, 1959– 2. Gamblers—United States—Biography. 3. Gambling. I. Title.

HV6710.3.R64 2010

363.4'2092—dc22

[B]

                2009036797

Interior design: Jonathan Hahn

Published by Chicago Review Press, Incorporated

814 North Franklin Street

Chicago, Illinois 60610

ISBN 978-1-56976-247-9

Printed in the United States of America

5 4 3 2 1

For gamblers everywhere.
May all your bets come through.

Acknowledgments

Thanks to Robert and Margaret Roeper, Lynn and Nick Zona, Bob and Colleen Roeper, Laura Roeper, Sam Saunders, Laura LeQuesne and Tim Filipiak, John LeQuesne, Emily Roeper, Caroline Roeper, and Bobby Roeper.

Thanks also to Bill Adee, Grace Adee, Leslie Baldacci, John Barron, Bruce Billmeyer, Michael Cavoto, Richard Cavoto, Michelle Carney, Jennifer Ciminillo, Don Dupree, Roger and Chaz Ebert, Laura Emerick, Robert Feder, Don Hayner, Paul Johnson, Alexandria Liberatore, Todd Musburger, Brian Musburger, Steve Pallotto, Phil and Jennie and Zachary and Jane Rosenthal, Shemp, Tony Svanascini, Jenniffer Weigel, Joyce Winnecke, Paige and Jim Wiser, and the American Eagle team.

Big thanks to my assistant, Lia Papadopoulos, her husband Sam, and their two boys, Konstantino and Christos.

Special thank you to Sarah Cooley. Pretty, yes. Wicked, never.

Major thank you to the Hammond Horseshoe Casino and their excellent PR and casino staff.

Thanks to the Basement Poker Crew, in particular our hosts, Brandy and CZ.

Thanks to Tim King, who believes "aggressive poker is winning poker," and is always in search of "a good old-fashioned double-up."

A special thank you to my editor, Yuval Taylor, for nurturing this project and for coming up with many suggestions and questions that made the story stronger. Thanks also to Devon Freeny, Mary Kravenas, and Laura Di Giovine at Chicago Review Press.

As always, big hugs for Sheree Bykofsky (I hope to be her equal at the poker tables some day) and Janet Rosen.

Introduction

We begin with a dream.

Because when you are a gambler, even though you don't believe in luck or trends or patterns, sometimes you just have to believe in dreams.

The dream hits you at three o'clock in the morning, and as you tell the story now, you're 100 percent solid sure of that time because the dream—the vision, the epiphany—lifted you right out of your sleep and into real-world consciousness on this pitch-black rainy night in Chicago, woke you with such force and clarity you're surprised the woman in bed next to you was still sleeping, blissfully unaware of what just happened. You almost expected her to be awake and whispering: *"I saw it too."*

She didn't. She doesn't. She just keeps sleeping, perfect in her beauty, blissful in her young life, untroubled by the gambler's worries

because she has no interest in the lure of the bet. (There are two types of people in this world: gamblers and the sane.)

In the dream, you are at Churchill Downs for the Kentucky Derby, at a lavish party populated by beautiful people in ridiculously brimmed hats and outfits the colors of Easter eggs. (In real life, just a few days later, Michael Jordan shows up at the 2009 Kentucky Derby in a suit so yellow it makes you blink. You see him on TV and you wish someone would ask him where Curious George is.) Even though you've worked in the entertainment field for years and you've met hundreds of the world's most famous people, you almost never dream about celebrities (although you once went horseback riding with Julia Roberts and you're almost positive that was an exclusively dream-world experience), yet at this Kentucky Derby Dream Party, you see a number of stars, including Penelope Cruz and Scarlett Johansson, and, hey, why not those two instead of Kathy Bates and Abe Vigoda, no offense to Kathy Bates and Abe Vigoda.

In the dream, the Kentucky Derby has just ended. The crowd is still buzzing.

And the tote board is flashing the numbers of the winning horses.

For whatever reason, you see only the numbers of the first two horses, in the exact order of finish. That's OK; you can live without knowing who's going to take third. The numbers are as bright and as clear in the dream as they would be in real life. So bright and clear that when you wake up from this dream, those digits seem to be floating in the air in front of you, so close you feel as if you could grab them and put them in your pocket. You don't feel the need to reach out across the sleeping beauty to grab your iPhone and make a techno-note, because there is no way in this world you're ever going to forget those numbers.

Ever.

It's the Tuesday night/Wednesday morning before the 2009 Kentucky Derby, and you have just literally dreamed up the winning numbers. You settle back under the covers, and the brunette turns in her sleep and murmurs, a half-smile emerging as her hair falls over her face. You're stone-cold awake, but you close your eyes, and you smile a bit as well. So much for handicapping the Derby. There's no way you're not going to bet those dream numbers; of course it doesn't mean the results are preordained or that you have any special psychic powers, but what if those numbers came in and you *didn't* have them? You'd be kicking yourself for life, and that would leave a bruise.

Tomorrow you will share your vision with your virtual friends on Twitter and Facebook. Thus you will have committed to the vision, and you will have a social-network record of the epiphany.

If this dream comes true, you'll have the story of a lifetime. Not to mention a huge spike in the bankroll.

On a sunny Saturday afternoon in May, the overflow crowd at the Stretch Run on LaSalle Street in Chicago has spilled onto the sidewalk, where they've set up wrought-iron tables and chairs and even an outdoor betting window if you'd like to walk up and make your picks and then continue on with your day. Inside, the spacious, multi-tiered off-track betting (OTB) facility is packed with one of the largest OTB crowds anywhere in the country. Unlike some OTBs, which are so forlorn and musty you expect to see somebody sweeping up lost souls along with the discarded tickets, the Stretch Run is a gleaming, well-lit, energetic joint that looks like your favorite oversized sports bar—if your favorite oversized sports bar had legal wagering available on every track in the country, and a few tracks outside of the country as well.

A small percentage of the crowd is going with the full-metal Derby wardrobe. Playing dress-up and getting into the mood, even though we're about 270 miles from Churchill Downs. A friend of mine texts and says she's upstairs at the Stretch Run, and I invite her to come downstairs and say hello to my group. Moments later my friend swoops into our section with four or five girlfriends, and they're all

wearing the dresses and the big hats because they've come from a more formal party, but it was relatively tame and they wanted to be part of a more energetic crowd. I'm happy to see her, really I am. So she's standing right in front of the monitor where a preliminary race has just gone off—a race on which I've wagered $200—and her mad saucer of a hat is obscuring the entire screen. So what? It's not as if watching the race will affect the outcome. I try my best not to try to look around the hat and at the monitor as we catch up on life.

Most of the crowd is dressed casually, as if at a baseball game—and speaking of baseball, there's Cubs manager Lou Piniella leaning against a railing just inside the main entrance, fresh off the Cubbies' 6–1 victory over the Florida Marlins earlier today. Wearing a denim shirt and jeans, a pair of reading glasses perched on his nose, Piniella looks like your crusty but funny uncle as he wields his pen and peruses the racing form. This is sports-mad Chicago, where fans recognize second-string catchers and assistant coaches on the street. People know that's Lou Piniella over there, but they're just treating him like a regular guy. Nobody's asking for cell phone photos or autographs. I'm told Piniella was offered a private room or a reserved table upstairs, but he declined, saying he wanted to hang in the main area and soak up the atmosphere.

My friend Michelle and I thread our way through the masses and meet up with a couple of my buddies: Teen, who has been known to place a wager or two, and MC, one of my poker pals. (Teen's real name is Steve, but he will forever be known as Teen because back in the college days, we were all 20 and 21 and he was still 19. When we're 88 and he's 86, we'll still be calling him Teen.) A staffer hands us a stack of programs and racing forms and leads us to our reserved table against the wall, with a great view of the multiple banks of TV monitors.

The Stretch Run is owned in part by Billy Marovitz, a local power broker who is married to Christie Hefner, daughter of Hef. Clad in a colorful sweat suit that makes you want to say, "Del Boca Vista!" Billy comes over and gives a hearty hello, asks us if we need anything, and offers to consult with some of the experts on hand to see if they've got any last-minute tips, especially with the track at Churchill Downs looking a little mushy from the rain.

No need for that, I say. I know who's going to win. It came to me in a dream. Billy laughs and claps me on the back. I'm sure he's heard 'em all before.

My friends know about the dream. At this point they're probably a little sick of hearing about the damn dream. They're going to make their own selections, but they're going to take a little bit of action on the dream horses as well. In the immortal words of the promoter in the first *Rocky* movie, "It's the chance of a lifetime. You can't pass it by!" A few other patrons at Stretch Run have seen my Twitters and my blog entry about the dream. One woman wishes me good luck and says she's got $20 on my combination. A guy in a Bears hat says, "Rich, if your horse wins, I'll eat my ticket. You got no chance, buddy. You should be betting on Pioneer of the Nile." I tell him to order some Tabasco sauce. It'll add a little flavor to his ticket.

Our waitress is paying tribute to the Derby by wearing a straw hat with some sort of plastic fruit on the brim. I believe the black lace bra peeking out from her tank top is just a personal choice. We order up Bloody Marys, beers, appetizers. For a few minutes my friends glance at the Derby charts and the predictions in the newspapers and in the Daily Racing Form, making comments and marking notations—but of course I already know the horse I'm betting to win, and the horses I'm boxing in my exacta.* While everyone else makes their Derby day calculations, I'll just bet a few of the races at other tracks. No need for me to read up on the Derby entrants today!

One bit of breaking news regarding the big race: the morning favorite, I Want Revenge, has been scratched—further paving the way for my upset special, right? That my horse is a super long shot,

---

* In order to win an exacta, you must pick the first- and second-place finishers of the race in precise order. Boxing the exacta costs twice as much, but if your picks come in first and second, regardless of the order, you win.

that not one reputable handicapper in the country has mentioned my horse as a candidate to even finish in the money, does not deter me in the least. I'm just glad I didn't dream about some 5-2 semifavorite winning it all. Where's the romance and excitement in that? I don't care what the experts say; I believe.

Time to make my bets. I work my way through the crowd, past the seriously long lines at the betting machines, and I head upstairs, where the human tellers are stationed. The line at the $100 window is only four or five deep, and moving quickly. I pull out a wad of hundreds and put $800 on my horse to win, along with a $100 exacta box on the two numbers that came to me in the dream. *Ba-CHEE ba-CHEE ba-CHEE*—the register spits out the tickets in increments of $150. As I tuck the tickets away and press my way back downstairs, I can't help but do a little fantasy calculating as I see the latest odds flashing on the screen. The "win" bets alone will net me in excess of $30,000. If the exacta comes in, that could be a hundred grand.

As post time approaches, the buzz in the Stretch Run grows louder. Every track in the country takes a break during the Derby, so every monitor in the joint is tuned to the telecast as the 19 horses are in the gate and ready to go.

"And they're off in the Kentucky Derby!" calls Tom Durkin, the veteran thoroughbred announcer for NBC. "And it's Join in the Dance who's racing for the lead, Musket Man has some early speed on the inside, Regal Ransom with some speed as well, beneath the twin spires for the first time. . . ."

Less than two minutes later, they're around the turn and heading for home, with Join in the Dance and Pioneer of the Nile and Regal Ransom jockeying for the lead. . . .

And then, something amazing happens—something that catches even Durkin by surprise. He's still calling the names of the aforementioned three horses when a long shot comes blazing out of nowhere on the rail, blowing by everyone else in the stretch. Durkin actually stops himself as he tries to figure out which horse is in the process of shocking the world, and by the time he calls this horse's name, the

race is essentially over and he can't suppress a chuckle as we all bear witness to perhaps the greatest upset in the history of the Kentucky Derby. . . .

When I was 11 years old, I made my first bet. I was on the playground at St. Jude the Apostle in South Holland, Illinois, in the requisite uniform of brown slacks, white shirt, and dark clip-on tie, and some older kid was talking about the upcoming Muhammad Ali–Joe Frazier fight, and how Ali was a traitor to his country and Frazier was going to kill him. I liked Muhammad Ali—I always favored the ultra-cool rebel athletes, like Ali and Connie Hawkins and Walt "Clyde" Frazier and Marvin "Bad News" Barnes and Dick "Don't Call Me Richie" Allen—and I thought the great Ali would win and I said so, and this older kid said, "Oh yeah? You wanna *bet* on it?" and without hesitation I said sure, I'll bet on it. As I recall, the bet was for five bucks, which is about all the money you have to your name when you're 11. Unless you're a child star.

On March 8, 1971, Frazier and Ali squared off at Madison Square Garden in the most widely anticipated heavyweight championship fight in at least a quarter century. If you wanted to see the fight, you had to pay to watch it in a movie theater on closed circuit TV. (Actor Burt Lancaster was one of the color commentators for the fight, and Frank Sinatra was the official photographer, I kid you not.) Nobody in my world was going to see the fight live at a pay-per-view theater. You'd have to wait to hear the results on the radio, or you'd see a report on the late news, with the sports guy reading a description of the fight accompanied by still photographs from the Associated Press. (The fight would be shown in its entirety on ABC's *Wide World of Sports* a week or two later.) I later learned Ali won most of the early rounds, but Frazier kept battling, eventually knocking Ali down in the 11th round. On the night of the fight, all I knew was what I heard on WCFL-AM when some DJ barked, "This just in: Frazier

beats Ali!" as he talked up the next record. That's how I found out I had lost the bet.

Five bucks! I felt like crying.

I was officially 0-1 as a gambler, down $5. I'm not sure I've ever made it back to the break-even point since then.

About a half-dozen years passed before I would make another bet. In high school, I started playing poker with my friends, betting a little bit on sports via something called parlay cards, learning about craps games, and otherwise getting involved in games of chance and skill and risk. Betting gave me an instant high. In the space between the placing of the wager and the moment when I learned the outcome—whether it was a three-hour sporting event or a quick roll of the dice—I felt a kind of euphoria. It was a combination of anticipation and anxiety. It made me feel alive.

Over the next four decades, I've experienced stretches of intense, life-consuming gambling—and I've gone years without making so much as a single bet. If that sounds like a drinker or a drug addict describing his ups and downs while trying to remain sober, well, maybe so. I'd like to think (rationalize?) I don't have a gambling problem, but I'll readily acknowledge I do have gambling *tendencies*.

As much as I love the bet, I'm equally fascinated by the gambling culture. All the games you can play, all the characters you can meet, all the chances you can take. For the last couple of years, I've wondered what it would be like to do with gambling what Morgan Spurlock did with his film *Super Size Me*—only instead of eating nothing but fast food every day for a month, I would indulge in one form of gambling or another every day for a month. When I had a window of opportunity in spring 2009, I leapt at the chance.

The self-imposed rules:

- Each and every day for 30 straight days, I would risk at least $1,000 total on some form of gambling.
- If I managed to double the bankroll at any point, the minimum risk would be increased to $2,000 every day.

- At one point I'd have to risk at least 25 percent of the bankroll on a single sporting event, poker tournament, roll of the dice, or hand of blackjack.
- If I reached a certain profit level, I would donate a percentage of the proceeds to charity.
- It wouldn't have to be a different form of gambling every day, but I did come up with more than a dozen variations, including craps, blackjack, slots, off-track betting, a major poker tournament in Las Vegas, online poker, the lottery— and, yes, the flip of a coin. Most of the gambling would take place in the Chicago area, but I planned on making journeys to Las Vegas, Michigan, Indiana, and Wisconsin. (You have not lived until you've spent a Monday afternoon at the greyhound track in Kenosha.)

And, because I was the one making the rules, I would reserve the right to adjust those rules as I went along—which is what led me to that Kentucky Derby bet, which we'll return to later in the book.

As I chronicle my daily adventures, I'll also flash back to some of the highlights and lowlights of my gambling life, and I'll tell some of my favorite stories and introduce you to a few of the characters I've met along the way.

You'll also hear about:

- What it's like to bet money you don't have on football games, knowing that if you lose, you're in some serious trouble.
- The worst referee's decision in the NFL in the last decade, and how it cost me thousands of dollars.
- An alleged killer who might have been motivated by a gambling problem.
- The time I won more than $20,000 on a single horse race.
- The college football fan I know who travels to Vegas once or twice a season to make one big bet on his golden lock selection of the year.

- What it's like to play in a celebrity poker tournament, alongside world champions such as Phil Hellmuth, Joe Hachem, and Erik Seidel and celebrities like Ben and Casey Affleck, Ray Romano, and Charles Barkley.
- Why the slots are such a bad play, why I hate baccarat, and why state lotteries are worse than any numbers game run by the mob.

The true national pastimes aren't baseball and football and basketball.

The real national pastime is fantasy football. It's March Madness and all those brackets. It's poker and slots and the lottery and craps and blackjack and keno and church raffles and Bingo. It's gambling.

Let the games begin.

Day 1

**Status:
Dead even**

"A gambler is nothing but a man who makes his living out of hope."
—*William Bolitho*

Go Radford! Beat North Carolina!
Well. Let's not kid ourselves. We all know Radford isn't going to beat UNC. I just want them to lose by 26 or fewer points. That would not constitute a "moral victory." It would constitute an "I'm really glad I bet on Radford" victory.

Oh, yeah, I'm a big Radford fan, from way back when. Like six minutes ago. Not that I'm entirely sure where Radford is located (I'm thinking it's Virginia or maybe Alabama), what their team nickname is (I'm thinking they're probably not the Radford Radicals, but they could be the Radford Rebels or the Radford Renegades), or whether it's Radford U., the University of Radford, Radford College, Radford

A&M, or the Radford School of Beauty and Hair Design.* I just know I need Radford and a bunch of other college hoops teams to beat the spread.

Now, this doesn't mean I don't appreciate how cool it must be for Radford to be in the NCAA, going up against one of the most storied programs in all of sports. Nor does it mean I wouldn't love it if Radford somehow pulled off the upset of the decade. If they were leading in the second half, fans across the country would be texting, Twittering, calling one another, saying, "Are you watching this game!" Even when I'm betting, I maintain my fan's interest in the game. But I can't pretend I woke up this morning with any keen insights into the Radford basketball program. I just believe in taking huge underdogs in the early rounds, because the spread is often stretched in favor of the powerhouses.

So approximately three minutes into my monthlong adventure, I'm breaking the law.

This is the thing about gambling in America: it's a maze of inconsistencies. You start talking about what's legal and what's illegal and what falls somewhere in between, and you'll wind up sounding a little like Samuel L. Jackson describing Amsterdam's marijuana laws in *Pulp Fiction.* ("It's legal but it ain't a hundred percent legal . . . it's legal to buy it, it's legal to own it, and if you're the proprietor of a hash bar, it's legal to sell it. . . .")

Across much of the country, you're encouraged to play the lottery and you can bet on horse racing. It's pure gambling—you're risking money on which horse can go the fastest around a track, or you're trying to predict which spinning, numbered balls will be spat into a

---

* My ignorance about Radford should in no way reflect poorly on the school itself. Radford University, founded in 1910, is a liberal arts school located between the Blue Ridge and Allegheny Mountains in southwestern Virginia. It is a fine school. The Radford athletic teams are known as the Highlanders. Among Radford's notable alums is actress Jayma Mays, whose credits include *Glee, Red Eye,* and *Paul Blart: Mall Cop.* Go Highlanders!

tube—with the odds decidedly stacked against you. Yet it's 100 percent legal.

In many states, the interstates are peppered with billboards urging you to take the next exit to a nearby casino, where they're offering an all-you-can-eat buffet of food, as well as an all-you-can-bet smorgasbord of gambling opportunities: "The Loosest Slots in Connecticut!" "More Poker Tables Than Any Casino in the Midwest!" "We'll Take Your Money with a Smile!"

Although I think I just imagined seeing that last one.

Yet if you're hosting a basement poker tournament, or if you've got a couple of cash video poker games in your corner tavern, or if you're placing or taking bets on the Super Bowl—well, sir, you are a scoundrel and an outlaw, and local and federal authorities can and occasionally will break down your door, confiscate the evidence, put you in cuffs, and haul your ass to the station, where you'll be fingerprinted and booked like a common criminal. Oh, and by the way: they've given your name to the local media, because they love to publicize the ongoing effort to combat the scourge that is illegal gambling.

The governmental hypocrisy on gambling is breathtaking. Consider my lawbreaking activities on a Thursday morning in March in Chicago: Today is the first day of the NCAA Division I men's basketball tournament, a.k.a. March Madness. For the basketball junkie, it's one of the most exciting sports days of the year, with the first games starting before noon and the last games ending after midnight. From New York to Ohio to Texas to California, it's wall-to-wall college hoops.

Every year in mid-March, tens of millions of Americans fill out their brackets in the hopes of winning the local office pool or maybe even one of those ginormous contests offered by ESPN, Yahoo!, Sports Illustrated, and CBS, among others. Whether you're a hardcore hoops junkie who knows about the bench strength of Sienna or a casual fan who picks North Carolina because powder blue is your favorite color and it makes you smile and twirl about, you cough up your 10 bucks, you fill out your brackets, and you spend the next three weeks tracking your progress.

Usually the guy running the pool is an anal-retentive superfan who sends out periodic updates listing every participant's point totals and the maximum number of points they're eligible to accumulate. By some great cosmic rule, the anal-retentive superfan never wins.

The big online pools have a computerized scoring system, capable of spitting out the rankings of literally millions of entrants in frighteningly timely fashion. No doubt those programs were designed by anal-retentive superfans.

Over the last couple of days, I've filled out a half dozen brackets. One of my friends has also set up a private, invitation-only pool via CBSSports.com. (CBS is in the middle of an 11-year, $6 billion contract to carry all the NCAA men's tournament games. Yet if an amateur college athlete signs with an agent or accepts a free suit of clothes, that player will be stripped of his or her eligibility.) You get an e-vite, you sign up, you fill out your brackets—and you're ready to compete with everyone else who was invited to join the private pool. It's up to you if you're going to do this for fun or for cash. The CBSSports.com computer doesn't ask questions; it just keeps track of everything for you and your friends, and sends out periodic updates.

My guess: approximately 1.2 percent of all participants in NCAA pools do so for fun, with no payouts to the winners. The rest of us are doing it for bragging rights and for cash money.

The CBS site also has their own bracket challenge, open to the world, and they receive literally millions of entries for that baby. One lucky winner out of the two million or more entries will take home a $10,000 prize.

Ah, but this isn't a gambling pool—that would be illegal and just plain wrong. It works like this: anyone who finishes in the top 10 percent is eligible for a drawing for the 10 grand.

"NO PURCHASE NECESSARY," state the contest rules. "The 2009 CBSSports.com Bracket Challenge (the 'Sweepstakes') is a competition based on the results of the 2009 Division 1 Men's College Basketball Tournament . . . the grand prize . . . will be awarded to a randomly-selected participant who is among the top 10 percent of point scorers in this Sweepstakes."

Get it? If you're running an office pool and you collect $20 from 25 coworkers and dispense cash to the top three finishers, you're breaking the law. (Though it's highly, supremely unlikely the feds are going to come after you.) But if you're a media giant with a multibillion-dollar contract with the NCAA and you conduct one of the world's largest bracket pools, now that's a *sweepstakes*. Perfectly harmless!

So silly. Why not award a major cash prize to the one individual who has the best score, instead of lumping the top 10 percent into a drawing? Why not reward the skill (and of course luck) one must possess in order to be *the* best out of millions of entrants?

Because somehow that would be against the law, whereas randomly choosing one name out of a pool of the top 10 percent is deemed good ol' All-American Fun. If anyone can explain the logic of that to me, I'm at rroeper@suntimes.com. I'll wait for my answer. I won't hold my breath. Or anything else.

So if you're wondering if I feel even a twinge of ethical doubt because some of my gambling activities aren't always considered legal by the current laws of the state and the nation?

Don't bet on it.

For decades it was against the law to bet on sports outside the state of Nevada—but finding a bookie anywhere in America is only slightly more difficult than finding a store where they'll sell you a lottery ticket. (In 2009, Delaware became the second state to legalize sports wagering.) Since I was 16, there's never been a time when I didn't know a bookie or two—or at least somebody who knows a bookie or two. Maybe you're not a sports gambler, and you're thinking, *I don't know any bookies*. Even if you've never bet on a football or basketball game in your life and you don't know anyone who's a regular gambler, I'll bet you know somebody who knows somebody. If you wanted

to bet $50 on a game taking place tonight and you asked everyone in your life if they knew anyone who could help you with that, odds are someone would be able to hook you up. You might not come into contact with an actual bookie, but somebody will say, "I can place that bet for you."

There was a time when I was betting on sports far too frequently, with all too predictable results. Hurts in the chest a little just to think about it. I remember sneaking upstairs during a huge Thanksgiving party and snooping around until I found a bedroom with a television set, so I could check on the game. (This was in the pre-Internet, pre–cell phone application days. Now you can check scores on your mobile device without leaving the room.) Less than two minutes to go and my team is driving for the win—and the win against the spread. Dinner is about to be served and people are calling my name, I'm sure it's a warm and fuzzy scene downstairs—and I'm cursing under my breath because there's another timeout on the field. There's no way I'm heading down to dinner until this thing is settled.

Finally my team lines up for an attempt for the game-winning field goal, and I stand a foot away from the screen with my hands on my knees, trying to will that ball through the uprights—and it's not even close. The ball skips harmlessly through the end zone, having landed a full five yards shy of the mark. I lose. Now I've got to sneak back downstairs and enter the dining room all smiles, as if I didn't just drop $200 I don't really have on this fucking Turkey Day game.

That was a couple of lifetimes ago. I learned, and then I learned again, and then I learned yet again—you can't beat the bookie. In recent years I've restricted my sports event wagers to the casual fan staples: the Super Bowl; a couple of low-stakes wagers while in Vegas and we were all betting the same team so we could scream at the big screen like maniacs; a bet on my Chicago White Sox when they were in the World Series. But in prepping for the book, I knew I'd want to bet on multiple games—so I called up an old friend who still dabbles in the occasional sports wager and asked him if the bookie we had back in the day was still in business.

The bookie—we'll call him Sid, because that sounds more like a bookie's name than Joaquin or Zac or Tila Tequila—has to be close to 60 by now. My old friend introduced me to him about 20 years ago. Sid is married, or at least he was married when I last talked to him seven or eight years back, and he has a couple of kids who are probably out of the house and on their own. He's a college graduate with a full-time, legit business, but he and a couple of partners have been running a bookmaking operation since the late 1980s. They don't take bets from just anyone; all of their clients are people they know or someone who has been brought in by a longtime customer.

Sure enough, Sid was still in business, and he told my friend he'd be glad to take my action once again.

We're long past the era in which bookies kept records in notebooks or on slips of paper that would dissolve in water if the cops showed up. Here's how it works in the 21st century—or, at least here's how it works with Sid.

You almost never have an actual, live conversation with Sid. It's all about the voice mail. (Sid pays cash for disposable phones with prepaid minutes, so even if someone tracked a call, there's no phone bill, nothing that can be traced back to him.)

You're given two telephone numbers. If you call the first number, you get a recorded message that goes something like this:

"It's March 30, and here are the morning lines, for news matter only. Pittsburgh is −11½ and 145 against Xavier, Arizona is −9½ and 134 vs. Cleveland State, LSU is −2 and 127½ against Butler . . . the next update is at 2 p.m."

The first number in the above example is the basic point spread. In other words, Pittsburgh is giving, or "laying," 11½ points to Xavier, meaning if you bet on Pitt, you have to win by 12 or more points to cover the spread. If you take Xavier, you're in effect winning by a score of 11½–0 before the opening tipoff. Even if Pitt wins 81–70, you're the winner because Xavier covered the 11½ point spread, losing by only 11. (This is why you see fans in sports bars or at games hooting and hollering near the end of a contest that seems to be well

in hand for one team. It's not the hot wings or the beer that has 'em screaming. The point spread is still in question.)

The second number is the over/under. I don't know who invented the over/under, but it's been around since long before I started gambling, and it was no doubt dreamed up by a bookie looking for another way to separate the bettor from his or her money, and as such it's a stroke of genius. The over/under is the total number of points scored by both teams. (You can also make over/under bets on an entire season—e.g., the over/under on the Cubs for the 2009 season was 91 wins. They finished 83-78, so if you took the "over," you lost.) If you don't have a rooting interest or a strong feeling about either team in a game, there's always the over/under. Take the "over" and you spend the whole game cheering for both teams to score like crazy; take the "under" and you're like the anti-Noonan faction in *Caddyshack*, rooting for everyone to "*Miss! Miss, miss, miss, miss, miss!*"

Once you get the latest lines from the recorded message, you make your picks and you call a second number. After the tone, you state your name, or your alias, or the numeric code you've been assigned—and you give your picks.

Let's say my code was 7777. (It wasn't. But let's say it was.) I call the hotline and say, "This is 7777. I'll take Pittsburgh for a dollar, the 'under' in the Pitt game for a dollar, and I'll take two dollars on LSU."

A "dollar" is a hundred dollars. If I wanted to bet $1,000, I'd say a "dime." It's all very Nathan Detroit.

Sid, or somebody working for Sid, periodically checks the messages and then keeps track of the wagers through whatever means he uses—probably some computer program disguised as a fantasy league. No doubt he knows the exact balance for each of his 60 or so clients. No doubt he also maintains that information in a way that leaves little or no evidence he's conducting a bookmaking operation.

Of course, there has to be some human contact at one key juncture—when it's time to pay up or get paid. It's not as if you can settle your debt by giving Sid your American Express number, though I'm sure there are some bookies that use PayPal or some other electronic method to make and take payments. Nor are you going to write a check or get paid by check. Bookmaking is still largely a cash operation. (Unless you're an Internet betting site, and even then they've got a way to make cash play.)

Let's not worry too much about the payment arrangement I have with Sid. Suffice it to say, neither one of us is worried about it—and the chances of me and Sid meeting face to face in some parking lot for a cash-in-an-envelope exchange, as I did a few times way back when (it was so long ago my car was a Camaro), are about as strong as #16 seed Morehead State's chances of beating #1 seed Louisville straight up in the opening round of the NCAA tournament.

For my opening bets, I take:

- LSU −2 Butler
- Over 127½ in the LSU-Butler game
- Texas A&M +3 BYU

We'll dip just our toes into the pool to start. A mere $100 on each game, and a three-bet parlay—which means I've got $100 on all three bets winning, in which case I'd net another $500. If I go 0-3, 1-2, or even 2-1, I lose the parlay bet outright.

CBS is carrying the games live, either on broadcast TV or on their Web site, where you can watch every game in real time, which in effect gives me four little TV monitors on my Mac desktop as I continue to do other work on my two laptops. (How many millions of office workers are keeping one eye on their NCAA picks as they perform their workplace duties at the computer?)

Texas A&M is the #9 seed in their region, and they're a slight underdog to #8 seeded BYU in this opening round game, but they're in control of the game throughout and they win by 13. There's nothing better than having a comfortable lead and the cushion of the point spread on your side. I'm up 100 bucks! This is easy. I quit. End of my gambling adventure, and a lesson to be learned: if you win your first bet, make it your only bet and go home.

Just kidding.

I'd forgotten about how sweet it is to win a laugher. Watching Texas A&M cruise to that easy win over Brigham Young was about as stressful as sipping a lemonade in a restaurant and then having the waitress hand you $100 instead of the check. Thank you very much.

The LSU-Butler game provides another easy victory, at least when it comes to the over/under. I've got 100 bucks on both teams scoring 128 points or more—and with more than five minutes left in the game, the over/under is over. Literally. The "over" is one of the few bets in sports that can be decided beyond any doubt before the game has reached its conclusion. Once the combined score is 128, it doesn't matter how much time is left or what happens the rest of the game. They're not going to take points off the board. You'll have to wait until the game is over to cash your ticket, but your bet is a guaranteed winner. It's a little different with the "under." You could be on pace to win your bet by 20 points—but what if the game goes into overtime, and then another overtime? All of a sudden, that low-scoring game is 81–80, and your "lock" of a victory just turned into a tough loss.

In addition to my over/under bet, I've got LSU and I'm giving away just two points to Butler, so when the Tigers race out to a 13-point lead in the first half, I'm looking strong. But then Butler mounts a furious second-half comeback, with these college kids fighting with all they've got to keep alive their dreams of NCAA immortality, and they cut the lead to 2, and the Butler subs on the bench are going crazy, and their cheerleaders are leaping and clapping and waving their pom-poms, and the announcers are opening up the Cliche Box and crowing about March Madness, and I'm quickly reminded of how insane it is to risk grown-up money on a bunch of 19- and 20-year-olds who are just a year or two out of high school. The 13-point lead is erased, and Butler goes ahead, 54–53.

Shit. You don't want to be giving away points *and* losing on the scoreboard. It's like trying to get money from an ATM, only to learn there'll be no cash and, in fact, you've got a negative balance.

Maybe the boys from Butler have exhausted themselves with the comeback, as so often happens in basketball. A team will frantically climb back from a big deficit, only to find themselves so wiped out once the game is tied that they quickly fall behind again.

That seems to be what's happening here. The Tigers fight back and regain the lead, leading by as much as seven as the clock winds down, but now we're in that last-few-minutes zone where the game of basketball becomes a much more tense, and yet in some ways a much duller and more tedious, enterprise. No other sport can be affected in such a profound manner by intentional stoppages in play, whether through timeouts or fouls. The team that's behind keeps shooting three-pointers and then fouling; the team that's ahead tries to play tough defense without fouling. When the latter team has the ball, it's all about getting it into the hands of their best free-throw shooters. It's stop and go, stop and go, stop and go, interspersed with myriad timeouts where they cue the music and cut to yet another commercial. With 19.3 seconds left, the score is LSU 70, Butler 66. (I'm always calculating the point-spread math in my head, so for me the score is LSU 70, Butler 68.) Between the free throws and the timeouts, it'll take nearly 10 minutes of real time for those last 19.3 seconds to tick off the clock.

Butler commits a foul and LSU heads to the line. Their guy hits both free throws, putting LSU up by 6 in the game and by 4 against the spread. And this is the thing about the spread, the thing that'll drive you crazy if you bet on games all the time: except for the exceedingly rare situation in which a player has made a bet or is shaving points, those athletes out there and their coaches are reacting to the real score, not the point spread differential. Quite often they'll do something on the court that makes perfect sense in the context of the game, but will crush your heart if it affects your bet. A guy will be dribbling out the clock with the game well in hand, and he'll have a clear path to an uncontested layup that will give you a point-spread victory—but he'll just whip the ball into the stands or hand it to the ref as the clock runs out, rather than rub it in with a meaningless basket.

Butler races down the court, sets up for a three-pointer—and it's nothing but net.

Now the score is LSU 72, Butler 69. The real game is in jeopardy, and I've got a one-point lead against the spread. Remember, I've already won my over/under bet. The over/under was just 127½ points, and we're at 141 and counting. I also won my earlier wager, so my three-bet parlay is still alive.

Another foul, another stop of the clock. LSU back at the line.

First free throw is good. The game is a point spread tie. Second free throw . . . front of the rim, then against the backboard, then it drops in.

Now it's 74–69.

I'm alternately pounding the desk, whistling in approval, or cursing the action on the screen in front of me. I really hate gambling. Except for when I'm loving it.

Another desperation three-pointer from Butler, another miss— but they tip it on for a two-pointer, making the score 74–71. Jee-zuz Christ!

With 4.5 seconds left, Butler commits a foul and LSU is back at the line, shooting the double bonus. They miss the first free throw but hit the second, making it 75–71.

This is dangerous territory. It should take Butler most if not all of the 4.5 seconds to inbounds the ball and take a shot—but LSU isn't all that interested in trying to stop them. At best they'd like to slow them down a bit so the clock runs out. But they're not going to risk a foul that would give Butler a chance for a miracle four-point play, i.e., a long shot plus a free throw. Better to let them shoot an uncontested three or take a layup. Who cares if final score is 75–71, 75–73 or even 75–74, as long as you win?

Well. We already know the answer to that one.

So even though the game is almost certainly LSU's, if you've got a bet down, the entire game comes down to those last 4.5 seconds. Butler gets ready to inbound the ball, LSU lays back—and the Butler kid throws the ball away, right into the hands of an LSU Tiger, who runs out the clock. Sweet. I win the last of my three bets, which means I also win the parlay.

And just like that I'm up a total of $900. March Madness is here!

When I was 16 years old—a junior in high school—I was working at a part-time job that paid a whopping $4.25 an hour. On average I'd make about $80 a week, before taxes. Armed with my $50 or $60, I'd play in basement poker games, including a regular Saturday night game hosted by the older brother of a friend of a friend. Most of the players were guys in their late teens or early 20s who had jobs at nearby warehouses, factories, stores, or steel mills; there were a few ancient guys in their 30s who would show up from time to time. Guys so old they wore wedding rings.

We played seven-card stud, five-card stud, and draw. (This was long before the Texas hold 'em boom.) I was a master at nursing my meager bankroll, especially in the first hour or so. If I was card-dead or I ran into a couple of bad beats and I lost my 50 bucks, I'd thank the host and be on my way. It's not like I had mouths to feed or bills to pay. I was a kid, living at home. My folks probably thought I was blowing my money on sports magazines and the movies.

In the fall of 1976, I went on a winning streak, and it was a thing of beauty. For about six or seven straight weeks, I was catching cards, making great reads, pulling off bluffs, and getting lucky. My bankroll was up to nearly $1,000. I'd never seen that much money in my life. I kept the money in a sock drawer beneath a stack of *Playboy* magazines.

As the game broke up one night, an older guy—everybody called him Harry because he looked just a little bit like Clint Eastwood in the *Dirty Harry* movies—said, "I don't know how much you make in that job of yours or what kind of action you're into, but if you want to bet on football games, I can give you a number to call."

Hell yeah! Football, that was my real area of expertise. I actually played football. I was #82 on the Thornridge High School Falcons. I knew football, college and pro. Give me a year of betting on football, and I'd win enough to pay my way into USC!

That's how naive I was, if you spell *naive* s-t-u-p-i-d. I actually thought it would be easy to pick the winners.

As luck would have it—and rest assured, that's all it was—I had a couple of good weeks betting on college and the NFL. That was followed by a couple of really horrendous weeks. As my bankroll dwindled, I made the rookie mistake of increasing the amounts of my bets. My thought process went like this: *So I went 1-5 betting $50 a game—I can make it up on a Monday night game with a single $200 bet.*

That's the kind of mentality that will crush you. That's the kind of mentality that crushes gamblers every day.

On a Monday night in November, the Dallas Cowboys were playing the Buffalo Bills. I was down to my last hundred bucks. I could have bet $50 or $100 on the game—but I was so heartsick about blowing the nearly $2,000 in profit from just a few weeks back that I wanted to get back up in a hurry—so I put $500 on the "under." This game was some 30 years ago, but I remember it clearly: the over/under was 38.

To this day, I can't tell you what I was going to do if I'd lost that bet. I would have owed the bookies $450 (including the bookie's commission fee on the big wager), and I had only the $100 to my name. There's no way in the world I would have gone to my parents for the extra $350. They would have helped me out, but I wouldn't have been able to bear the disappointment and concern I'd have caused them. (Other than throwing in a couple of dollars on a Kentucky Derby or Indy 500 pool, neither my mother nor my father has so much as placed a bet in their lives. You'd be more likely to see my father walking on the moon than strolling through a casino.) I'm not saying the bookies would have chased me down after high school, thrown me in a car, and taken me to an alley to break my thumbs over $350—but they wouldn't have let me off the hook, either. They would have put me on some sort of payment plan, or they would have given me a deadline to come up with the money—and if I didn't make a payment or I failed to meet a deadline, there would have been consequences. They would have contacted my family, or, yeah, someone might have roughed me up a bit. This wasn't some corny short story. They weren't going to just say, "All right, we're going to let you slide, just this once. Lesson learned, young fella. Now get back to the business of being a teenager, and don't ever try to make a bet with us again!"

I couldn't watch the game. I mean I literally couldn't watch it. We had a hand-me-down color TV and a black-and-white portable in our house, and they were both taken that night by either my parents or an older sibling. Nobody else in the house had the least bit of interest in a Monday night football game that didn't involve the Bears, and I was supposed to be doing homework, so I couldn't go to a friend's house to watch the game. So I called the Sportsphone hotline for updates every half hour or so. (Before the days of ESPN and instant online updates, you'd call Sportsphone and get a recorded voice providing "the latest scores.")

The 1976 Dallas Cowboys were a powerhouse that would end the regular season with a record of 11-3; the Bills were a 2-12 joke. Didn't matter to me. I didn't care who won that Monday night game, as long as the total points scored was less than 38. I wanted fumbles and stalled drives and missed field goals and two-yard gains up the middle while the clock kept running.

Praise the Lord, it was a defensive struggle throughout. I never got an update that made my heart sink. As the night went on, my mood got lighter and lighter. When the Sportsphone guy announced the Cowboys-Bills game was a final, it was Dallas 17, Buffalo 10.

I had survived. My bankroll was back up to a whopping $600.

The brush with disaster didn't scare me enough to make me quit, but I did pull back the reins, at least for a while. For the remainder of the season, I never wagered more than $100 on a single game—and when I went broke, I stopped.

I had looked into the abyss, and I didn't want to risk a head-first plunge. At least not at the age of 16.

In the history of the 64-team format for the NCAA tournament (now 65 teams because of that silly "play-in" game) stretching back to 1985, there have been 100 games pitting a #1 seed against a #16 seed. The #1 seed has won every time. A #15 seed has won against a #2 seed just four times. When you're filling out your bracket and you're looking for upset, history suggests you take chances on first-round upsets by a #12 seed or maybe even a #13 seed—but it's folly to predict a monumental shocker. It just never happens.

Yet in two of the later games on my first day of betting, I take 16th-seeded Radford against #1 seeded North Carolina in a first round game, and I bet on #16 Tennessee-Chattanooga against #1 seed Connecticut in another first round game that has "blowout" written all over it.

Why? Because Radford is getting 26 points and Tenn-Chattanooga is getting 21½ points, and though neither team has a realistic shot at an upset, I figure perennial powerhouses UConn and UNC are coming off tough conference tournaments and might be a little worn down physically and emotionally, and they could be a little complacent for their first-round matchups against these nobodies. You get a relatively sloppy, low-scoring game, maybe a halftime score with the #1 seed leading 28–22 or something like that, and the underdog might stick around long enough to cover the spread. Even if it's a 30-point blowout with 10 minutes left in the game, the coaches of the favored teams might rest their starters rather than risk injury or appear to be piling on. You have a decent shot of stealing a point-spread victory during garbage time.

Besides, I know the average bettor has a hard time going against a North Carolina or a Connecticut in a first-round game, so I'm figuring the spread might be set a bit high, just to attract some action on the underdogs. (When bookies set the line, they're not saying they believe North Carolina is 26 points better than Radford. They're saying 26 is the number most likely to attract an equal amount of wagering on either side, thus lessening their risk factor. If there's the same amount of money bet on both teams, the bookie is guaranteed a profit, as he or she takes a 10 percent fee—called the vigorish, the "vig," or the "juice"—on every losing bet. You bet $100 and you win, you get $100. You bet $100 and you lose, you owe the bookie $110.)

I also parlay Radford with Tennessee-Chattanooga: if both bets come in, I'll get $260 for a $100 parlay, as you get 13-5 odds on a two-team parlay. But remember, if I go 0-2 or even 1-1, I lose outright. As you can see, there are multiple possibilities when one bets a parlay—and the only way you win is if all of your bets come through. That's why, as is the case with virtually every "exotic" bet ever offered by any bookie or any casino in the history of gambling, guess what? The odds are not in your favor.

I know. It's a shocker.

I also take Washington giving away 6 to Mississippi State as well as under 149 in that game; Illinois −5 against Western Kentucky; and UCLA giving 8½ to Virginia Commonwealth.

Also, I have Binghamton +25 points against everyone's favorite perfect team to hate, Duke. When Binghamton scores the first bucket of the game, I'm not up 2–0, I'm up 27–0, baby!

I feel like James Caan in the 1974 classic *The Gambler*, when he would bet ridiculous sums of money on games involving teams like Brown, listening to the games on his portable radio and simmering with rage when he'd lose. (Lauren Hutton, playing his girlfriend: "I don't understand any of it." Caan: "It's just something I like to do.") You can tell yourself there's something romantic and thrilling about this whole gambling thing—that you're following in the footsteps of Dostoevsky and his roulette addiction, the Earl of Sandwich, Chevalier de Mere, Bat Fucking Masterson. Maybe so. You're also just a guy betting on the likes of Radford and Binghamton and Tennessee-Chattanooga. And you've known more than a few women who have uttered that Lauren Hutton line to you: "I don't understand any of it."

North Carolina crushes Radford, 101–58.

UConn destroys Tenn-Chattanooga, 103–47.

So much for my massive-underdog theory.

Washington covers for me. I also win my over/under bet on that game. UCLA wins 65–64, meaning they advance to the next round but they're a loser for me, as I was giving away 8½. Ten minutes into the Illinois–Western Kentucky game, as the Illini brick shot after shot, I know that one's a dead bet. Not only do they fail to cover the spread, they lose the game outright.

My parlays are dead. The only late bright spot is the final score of the Duke-Binghamton game: Duke wins 86–62. I was getting 25 points and as it turns out, I needed every one of them. The boys from

Binghamton covered. Their season is over, but they're winners in my book.

When it all shakes out for the day, I've made about $2,000 in bets, and I'm up.

Just barely.

Day 2

**Bankroll:
+$50**

We start the day with three bets of $1,000 each.

The first wager is actually a stock purchase. I buy $1,000 worth of Citigroup stock at $2.81 a share. Let's face it, the stock market has always been a gamble, and never more so than in these dark economic times. Every time you click to a news site or turn to CNBC or flip through the business section of a newspaper—a newspaper that might be on its last legs—there's another story about a stock plummeting, or Bernie Madoff ripping off his clients, or a CEO taking a huge bonus as his or her company files for bankruptcy, or a Big Three automaker laying off even more workers, or the president's stimulus package.

A few words here about the ever-sensitive issue of money, the last taboo subject. (Celebrities that will gladly divulge all about their drug habits and their multiple lovers would be deeply offended if you asked them how much they make per movie.) When I announced

this project in my column and on my blog, I heard from a lot of folks who said it sounded like an interesting experiment—but I also heard from a few who said it was irresponsible for me to cavalierly wager thousands of dollars on games of chance at a time when so many people are out of work.

Understood. But first, I'm not gambling with your money; I'm gambling with *my* money. One should never risk money one can't afford on a roll of the dice, a turn of a card, or the outcome of a sporting event—but I've done just that on more than one occasion over the years, and I take full responsibility for it. Granted, my financial fortunes have shifted drastically in my favor over the years. I've been incredibly lucky to score some high-profile, lucrative gigs. But as I write these words, the newspaper for which I've written for the last 20 years has filed for bankruptcy, and every week there's a new rumor about us closing. In the summer of 2008, I walked away from the television show I cohosted for eight years because there was an executive in charge of the program who was hell-bent on dumbing down the show and destroying its legacy in the name of attracting more viewers. (It didn't work. Ratings are down by a large margin since my departure. I'd be lying if I said I didn't take some satisfaction in that— but I'm also frustrated that I had to walk away in the first place. Also, the economy got much worse shortly after I left the show, effectively killing a deal I had to return to the airwaves in the fall of 2008. In late 2009, I reached an agreement on a new show, to begin airing in fall 2010.) I'm not crying poor. I'm not saying my situation is in any way comparable to the plight of millions of Americans who have lost their jobs and are in danger of losing their homes, with little hope on the horizon. I'm not going to get into the particulars of my own financial obligations and the things I do for myself or for others with my cash. Suffice it to say it matters to me if I win or lose these bets. Money is still money to me.

I buy a thousand bucks' worth of the beleaguered Citigroup— which was trading for $56 a share a little more than three years ago—for that $2.81 a share price, as a nod to the economy and as an investment gamble. Ironically, it's probably not much of a gamble at this point. I know that unlike a $1,000 bet on a single sporting event or game of blackjack, there's very little chance I'll lose the entire $1,000—but there's also virtually no chance of doubling my money in 30 days.

I also bet $1,000 on the Chicago White Sox to win the 2009 World Series, at the bargain rate of 35-1. Do I really think my favorite team is better than the Red Sox, the Yankees, the Rays, the Phillies, the Dodgers, or the Cubs, among other preseason favorites? No. But the Sox did win their division last year, and they've got a potentially interesting mix of veterans and newcomers in their lineup. They're certainly better than a 35-1 shot—but unlike the Cubbies, they've never been a glamour team that attracts much betting action outside Chicago, so the price is nice.

The last of the three $1,000 bets is actually a bet about all my other bets.

When I went public with the premise of this book, I heard from one of my poker buddies, Mel Thillens.

"I'll bet you lose at least $15,000 over the 30-day period," said Mel.

"Thanks for the support," I said with a laugh.

"No, I mean I'll really bet you," said Mel. "I'll bet you $1,000 you lose at least 15 grand. There are too many days when you're guaranteed to lose. When you bet on the horses, the slots, when you buy lottery tickets—there's no way you're going to win on those days."

"You're serious? You want to make a real bet on this."

"Absolutely."

Done deal. So in addition to the daily bets, I now have three pending bets: on the stock market, the White Sox, and myself.

I was thinking about driving to Joliet, Illinois, this afternoon to do some casino gambling at the Empress—but then came this news bulletin from the *Chicago Tribune*:

A massive fire [has] destroyed much of the Egyptian-themed entrance building at the Empress Casino in Joliet, sending dark smoke that was visible for miles rising above the two towering pharaohs alongside the front door.

The blaze, which officials said might have been sparked by welders working on a kitchen duct system, started small about 10 a.m. But within hours more than half the city's Fire Department was working to prevent its spread to the casino barge, Fire Chief Joe Formhals said.*

So much for that idea. At least no one was injured in the fire. I take this as a sign I should be playing a little blackjack online instead of in a traditional brick-and-mortar casino, so I sign up for an account with Bodog.com, one of the larger and better known of the online gambling sites. They offer cash games and tournament poker; casino games, including craps, roulette, blackjack, and baccarat; virtual slot machines; bets on thoroughbred and harness tracks from across the country and around the world; sports wagering; and even prop bets on entertainment-related competitions, e.g., "Will Heather Mills lose her prosthetic leg at any point during *Dancing With the Stars*?"—and no, I'm not making that up. (More on prop bets later.)

Like more than a few online betting operations, Bodog has something of a checkered past and is plagued by legal ambiguities. In 2006 the United States government passed the Unlawful Internet Gambling and Enforcement Act, which stopped American banks from making transactions with online sites, most of which are based offshore or in obscure locales in Canada or Europe. Although this didn't make it illegal for American gamblers to play on the sites, they were no longer able to use a credit card to make deposits. Some online poker sites were driven out of business by this ruling. Others closed their

---

* The massive blaze caused some $340 million in damage. The feel-good silver lining in this story: the casino paid its workers in full during the renovation process—and many of those workers spent the downtime doing volunteer work in the community.

doors to American customers—but left those doors cracked open a bit for those willing to slip on through. Since 2006 there's been a lot of legal wrangling on both sides of the issue. By the time you read this, it might be perfectly legal for all sites to do business with American customers and American banks.

In the meantime, it's all a little hazy. (Later in the book I'll describe why if I want to play in some online tournaments, I have to send money to people I've never heard of in Costa Rica.) I sign up for an account with Bodog, not really certain how or even if I'll be able to make a deposit. Once I've an established an account, I click on the "Make a Deposit" option, and I'm given several options:

- Credit Card
- eWalletXpress
- Money Transfer
- Rapid Transfer
- Click2Pay
- Virtual Pin

Most of those methods involve setting up an account elsewhere online, depositing funds from a checking account, and then transferring those funds to Bodog. The credit card option works just like any other credit card payment plan you'd find at an online store: you give them all your information, you click on an amount, you press "Confirm," and there goes your money.

I give them an American Express account number and fill out all the necessary information, fully expecting to be told they are unable to process the transaction because of my United States address. But that's not what happens. Bodog quickly and happily accepts my deposit. Now I've got real money in the account and I'm free to bet on anything ranging from blackjack to the third race at Penn National. (There are other sites where you can watch video of virtually every horse race in the country in real time. Combined with the Bodog account, this in effect turns my home office into an

OTB facility that never closes. Yeah, that's not too dangerous for the gambler.)

I convert $500 in cash to $500 in Bodog casino chips and hit the virtual blackjack table. As I would do in a regular casino, I start out gently, with bets of $20 per hand.

Bodog blackjack action is even faster than you'd get if you were playing one-on-one with a live dealer. The "cards" come flying at you in rapid-fire fashion, and once the action is to the virtual dealer-bot, he turns over his cards (and hits his hand if necessary) and either scoops your money or pays out with such robotic speed it takes you a moment to absorb what just happened. *I have 20, he has 14! Oh wait, he just gave himself a 2 and then a 5 for a 21, that means I lose . . .*

After the first 27 hands, I'm up a little. Then I hit a bad streak:

Hand #28: I have 2-6, I get a Jack for 18. Dealer has a J, turns over a J for a 20.

Hand #29: I have 15, dealer gets J-5-2 for 17.

Hand #30: Dealer shows a 5. I get 16 and stick. Dealer turns an 8 and a 4 for 17.

Hand #31: Dealer shows a 4. I have A-7 and stick. Dealer turns over a 9 for 13, draws an 8 for 21.

Hand #32: Dealer gets 21.

Hand #33: I have 20. Dealer shows a 10. Turns a 3, then a 9, busts.

Hand #34: I hit on 12, get an 8 for 20. Dealer shows K, turns over 3—gets a 7 for 20.

Hand #35: I have 11. Dealer shows a 3. I double down. I get an 8 for 19. Dealer turns over an 8 for 11, gets a Q for 21.

Hand #36: I have 13. Dealer shows a 7. I hit and bust. Dealer had 13.

Hand #37: I have 11. Double down. I get 18. Dealer has 19.

Hand #38: I have 18. Dealer shows 20.

Hand #39: I have 17. Dealer gets a 20.

After 50 hands, I'm dead even. After 100 hands, I'm down just $30. I feel sufficiently warmed up and I'm comfortable with the Bodog graphics and the mechanics of betting, so I up the stakes to $50, $60, even $100 a hand.

That's when things get ugly. When I draw a strong hand like a 19 or a 20, the dealer matches my total or one-ups me. He deals himself 21, a lot. I also bust with alarming frequency.

Let's take a look at a sequence of 24 consecutive hands. (I did a screen capture of each hand and stored them on my computer so as to keep an exact record of what happened.)

Hand #1: Dealer shows K. I have 4-2 and then I get a Queen for a 16. I hit again and get the miracle 5 for a 21. The dealer has 15—and he gets a 6 for a 21. That's a push.

Hand #2: I get 18. Dealer has a 20.

Hand #3: I get 17, Dealer goes has a 6 and a 6 for 12. He draws a 9 for a 21.

Hand #4. I have a 20, Dealer busts.

Hand #5: I have 18, Dealer busts.

Hand #6: I get a 20. Dealer busts. Three in a row in my favor!

Hand #7: I have a 19 and the dealer shows 9-7 for an ugly 16. But he draws a 5 again, giving him 21. Again.

Hand #8: Dealer shows a Q. I hit a crappy hand and bust.

Hand #9: Dealer gets blackjack.

Hand #10: I get blackjack. So does the dealer.

Hand #11: Dealer busts.

Hand #12: Dealer busts.

Hand #13: Dealer busts.

Hand #14: I have 20. Dealer shows 21.

Hand #15: I have 19. Dealer has a total of 4. Hits once and gets a Queen. Hits again and gets a 6 for a total of 20.

Hand #16: Dealer busts.

Hand #17: I have 19. Dealer has 14. Gets a 2 for 16, then a 3 for 19. Tie.

Hand #18: Dealer gets blackjack.

Hand #19: Dealer busts.

Hand #20: I have a 19. Dealer gets a 20.

Hand #21: I bust.

Hand #22: I'm dealt an 11, but before I can even double down, Dealer gets yet another blackjack.

Hand #23: Dealer busts.

Hand #24: I have 12. Dealer gets 3-A-8-8 for 20.

So in 24 hands, the dealer pulled either a 21 or a 20 out of shitty cards a total of five times. He also dealt himself blackjack a whopping five times—that's more than 20 percent of the hands. I've got no chance against a run like that.

My bankroll is gone, so I replenish it with another $500. In less than an hour at the blackjack table, nearly all of that has been wiped out as well, in equally brutal fashion. I've been playing blackjack for 25 years, and I've experienced some incredible runs, some horrific losing streaks, and a lot of rollercoaster rides. I've rarely seen a dealer get so many blackjacks and turn so many underdog hands into winners, thanks to the draw of just the right card at just the wrong time (for me).

I want to make this crystal clear: I'm not saying Bodog is rigging the blackjack game to slant the odds heavily in its favor. I'm perfectly capable of losing $1,000 or more on blackjack in even less time at a real casino.

But I will say this: Over the course of this 30-day adventure, I return to the Bodog blackjack tables another half-dozen times, because I am stubborn, because I want to see if the odds will turn in my favor, and did I mention I'm stubborn? And I never get hot. I never get more than a couple of hundred bucks up. Time after time, Robot Dealer Man deals himself blackjacks and 20s and 19s. If that pattern held up and all I did was play Bodog blackjack every day for 30 days, I would have lost $100,000 or more, easily.

In addition to my blackjack adventure, I've got a few grand in sports bets out there, including these midday NCAA games:

- Arizona State −5½ Temple
- E. Tennessee State +22 Pittsburgh
- Cornell +14 Missouri
- Dayton +11 W. Virginia

Here's a Degenerate Gambler Special: you can actually bet on spring training baseball games, which often feature unknown players who will be nowhere near the major league roster when camp breaks. In the spirit of exploring as many gambling options as possible for the book, I put down $240 on the White Sox against the Giants in one of these practice games. It serves me right when the Sox get crushed 10–3. Why don't I just find a neighborhood T-ball game and see if I can get some action on that?

Now I'm watching the Missouri-Cornell game live on the CBS web site, and I can assure you if I didn't have money on this game, I would have little interest in watching a first-round NCAA game in the middle of a weekday afternoon.

Missouri is up by 12 with 3:03 to go. The game is pretty much over, but remember, I'm getting 14 points—so for the gambler, this game is far from decided. No doubt we're going to see a parade of three-point shots by the desperate Cornell and free throws by trying-to-ice-this-game Missouri.

By the way, this game is being played in Boise. As is often the case with these early-round games, the stands are half-empty. How many students can afford to make the journey from Columbia, Missouri, or Ithaca, New York, for one or two games?

More to the point, why is Mizzou heading to the rim for a dunk when they should be taking time off the clock! Another breakaway, another dunk, and suddenly it's a 16-point game. This nail-biter of a game (in terms of the spread) could quickly turn into a blowout if Cornell keeps missing threes and Missouri keeps taking it to the rim.

But then Cornell mounts a bit of a charge, cutting the lead to 73–57 with 1:35 left. After we miss a couple of three-pointers—and, yes,

I'm now saying *we* when I talk about friggin' Cornell—we get a tip-in basket to cut the lead to 14. Against the spread, this game is all tied up. Cornell is employing a full-court press, and for some reason Missouri keeps attacking the basket. Why is the coach not telling them to pass the ball around and take time off the clock? Speak up, man! They don't need more points, they need to get that scoreboard to read 00:00.

Mizzou misses a free throw but gets the ball back on a turnover. They're up by 17.

With 44.9 seconds left, Missouri commits a foul, which is like a gift from heaven for me. Cornell gets free throws *and* the clock is stopped. If you're betting on Missouri, you're wondering why in God's name Missouri would foul, when all they're trying to do at this point is run out the clock. Well, guess what: kids a year or two out of high school will sometimes make mental mistakes on the court.

Finally, *finally*, Missouri empties its bench and takes out the starters. Now you've got a bunch of scrubs out there who forget everything they've learned in practice and just want to get their hands on the ball so they can heave a shot and maybe get their name in the record books as having scored in an actual NCAA tournament game. Who can blame them?

Sure enough, one of the Mizzou benchwarmers sinks a shot and celebrates like he's Christian Laettner hitting a buzzer beater for Duke. That's it. I'm done. The final is Missouri 78, Cornell 59.

This is why I can't continue to watch all of these games live for the duration of the tournament. I'll have a bleeding ulcer. If I'd seen the result scrolling across the screen on ESPN, I'd just think it was another 5-point loss to the spread. Watching the flow of the action, with all the ups and downs and what-ifs and they-shouldas, will kill ya.

Later in the day, I place bets on Louisville, Ohio State, USC, Portland State, and Florida State. This is not optimum betting strategy. The more wagers you make, the more likely the odds will catch up to you. If you're betting $100 a game and you go 3-3, you lose $30 in vigorish. If you're betting $100 a game and you go 9-9, you have the exact same winning percentage of .500—but you'll have to pay the bookie $90 in commission fees. Not to mention it's a lot more difficult to go 8-4 when you've got 12 bets going than it is to go 2-1 on three games you've studied involving teams you've actually watched. So why am I doing it? Because I'm trying to win, but I'm also staying true to my past betting patterns. You're always trying to win when you gamble, but you do it for the jolt of excitement as well. The more games I bet, the more action I have.

When all the games have been played, I'm almost even with my sports bets for the day. Almost. But because of my deadly session at the Bodog blackjack tables, the day is painted with a big fat *L*.

"Hey, It Happens"

At one point I got so frustrated with the pounding I was taking on the Bodog blackjack tables, I fired off an e-mail to their support team, telling them I'd never experienced such a horrific run at a "real" blackjack table in my life.

A few days later I received a response:

"My name is Chris and I'm with the Bodog Live team here at Bodog. I was reviewing the action on last week's games and I noticed that it was a rough time for you. Hey, it happens, but I'd like to give you a chance to get back at it, on the house. Next time you open the Bodog Live console you'll find a $22 free bet in there.

"Remember, if you ever have any problems we're just a phone call away."

Really? Because I met this woman and we had a couple of great dates, but now she's not returning my texts. Can you help me with *that* problem?

Considering I had lost thousands of dollars when I received the e-mail, the offer of a free $22 bet was underwhelming. (Not that they owe me anything at all.) A free $100 casino chip in my account would have seemed like a solid goodwill gesture—and a smart move to get me back to the tables. But 22 bucks? That's the equivalent of having a bad run at the casino tables and getting handed a lukewarm beer as a consolation.

Day 3

Bankroll:
-$940

"The urge to gamble is so universal and its practice is so
pleasurable, that I assume it must be evil."
—*Heywood Broun*

It is said of the hardcore gambler that he or she will gladly bet you on a race between two raindrops trickling down a window. I'm not so sure two degenerates have ever literally stood at a window, betting on the rain—but I wouldn't doubt it. I've been in a bar with guys as they bet each other on whether the next woman to enter the joint would be a blonde, brunette, or redhead—which led to an argument about every two minutes, because an awful lot of women have a hair color somewhere between the basic shades. (It also gives you an excuse to approach a woman and say, "Excuse me, I was wondering if you could help me with this bet I made. . . ." And that usually leads to no success whatsoever.)

Tales of prop bets among big-time gamblers are legendary. "Prop" stands for "proposition," and a prop bet is any wager in which one gambler proposes a challenge to another. It can be anything from "I bet the next three cards out of the deck will all be diamonds" to "I bet you can't hold your breath for 90 seconds." In Michael Konik's *The Man With the $100,000 Breasts*, he writes of a man who gets breast implants—38C, as I recall—to win a bet. The same guy pledges to live in a hotel bathroom for 30 straight days because his buddies bet him $14,000 he couldn't do it. Halfway through the bet, his friends realize he's going to stick it out, so they pay him $7,000 to end it.

Howard Lederer, the older brother of 2009 *Celebrity Apprentice* runner-up Annie Duke and a poker pro known as "the Professor" because of his cerebral approach to the game, is a longtime vegan who nevertheless ate a cheeseburger—because he was offered a $10,000 prop bet that he couldn't do it.

Most likely the prop bet was invented on the same day the bet was invented. A couple of Neanderthals wagered on who could kill the next mammoth—and while they were chewing down, one Neanderthal challenged the other to go a week without eating any mammoth whatsoever.

In 1960 a British man found a bookmaker who offered him 1,000-1 odds against a man setting foot on the moon before January 1, 1970. The man placed a 10-pound wager in favor of the moonwalk. One hopes he sent a thank you note to NASA and Neil Armstrong in the summer of '69.

Poker pro and notorious prop bettor Huckleberry Seed (yep, that's his real name) denies the story that he once lost $50,000 to fellow pro Phil Hellmuth, who supposedly challenged Seed to stand in the ocean with water up to his shoulders for 18 hours. Seed says the bet was for $10,000 and he'd have to *float* in the ocean for 24 hours—which he was unable to do, even though he was allowed to wear a wet suit.

Amarillo Slim claims he once had a $40,000 bet that said he couldn't hit a golf ball at least a mile. Now, obviously there are ways to get around this challenge—e.g., driving a ball from an airplane—so a list of rules was drawn up. But Slim says he got around the rules and legitimately won the bet by driving the ball on a frozen lake, where it supposedly skidded for a mile and a half before rolling to a stop.

Mike "the Mouth" Matusow bet Ted Forrest $100,000 that Matusow could go from 241 pounds to his high school weight of 181. When it came time for the weigh-in, Matusow weighed exactly 180.8 pounds, good for a hundred grand.

You can also make prop bets on sports and even some entertainment and political events. We always hear a lot about prop bets in the week leading up the Super Bowl, when the Vegas bookmakers and the online sites offer odds on everything from the pregame coin flip to the length of "The Star-Spangled Banner" to whether or not there will be a safety in the game.

As I'm writing this, there's a veritable cornucopia of wacky prop bets available online. In most cases, they set a limit of a few hundred bucks on these wagers. (Nobody's going to let you plunk down $20,000 on the outcome of some reality TV show, especially one that's been pretaped.) I put $100 on Megan Joy to win season 8 of *American Idol*, but Joy is soon eliminated. (There is no Joy in Mudville—mighty Megan has struck out!) Adam Lambert is the overwhelming *Idol* favorite on every site, at odds ranging from 1-2 to 1-9, meaning you'd have to bet $900 just to win a hundred bucks on the guy. (NOTE: Lambert was eventually bested by Kris Allen in what many called the biggest upset in *American Idol* history. I didn't have any money on it, so I didn't care.)

In my great home state of Illinois, three former governors have been jailed since the 1970s—and that doesn't include our latest shamed gov, Rod Blagojevich, whose antics were so wacky during the winter of 2008–09 he was repeatedly lampooned on *Saturday Night Live* and his wife—his wife!—became a contestant on *I'm a Celebrity . . . Get Me Out of Here!* eating tarantula, nearly drowning, and dealing with the likes of Heidi and Spencer from *The Hills*. While facing multiple corruption charges, Blago went on a media blitz that would shame the Kardashians, appearing on *The View*, bantering with Let-

terman, squaring off with Larry King, and guesting on virtually every radio and TV show short of *America's Most Wanted*.

The online gambling site BetUS.com posted a number of prop bets on Blago's future, including:

Will he serve jail time?
Yes: 1-3
No: 100-1

Comes out of the closet in prison (reveals he is gay):
Yes: 1-1
No: 2-1

Next job will be:
Construction worker: 10-1
Pizza delivery guy: 5-1
Used car salesman: 1-1
Adult video actor: 1000-1
Motivational speaker: 13-1

You'd think they'd give you better odds on Blago becoming a used car salesman, as that's not much more likely than the "adult video actor" option. Then again, those odds on the ex-governor coming out of the closet look pretty good to me.

Troll around the Internet and you can find sites offering odds on who will become the next pope, which Major League Baseball player will next be suspended for a drug policy violation, and "Who's [sic] vagina is going to hit the web next?" (Halle Berry was 50-1, Madonna was 20-1, and Lindsay Lohan was just 5-1. Sure enough, a few weeks after I found that posting, Ms. Lohan's "fire crotch," as the online gossipers so delicately put it, was on display as she exited a limo.)

The sports sites also offer prop bets on games in progress—and that's where I'm at today. In the UCLA-Villanova game, I've got money on the halftime point total, on Villanova's Scottie Reynolds and UCLA's Darren Collision making their first field goal attempts, on whether or not the first basket of the game will be a three-pointer, on which team will score 10 points first—and a handful of other bets that are essentially tosses of the coin using real human beings as the coin. I mean, when Collison bangs his first shot off the back of the rim and it costs me an instant $110, am I supposed to think I should have known better? Would it really matter if I knew how often Collison makes his first shot of the game?

Reynolds misses his first shot. *Loss.*

First basket of the game is not a three-pointer. *Loss.*

I make another prop bet, on the Texas A&M–UConn game. I'm picking Texas A&M to get to 10 points first. When I check in on the game, UConn is leading 8–0. Suffice it to say the Aggies do not score the next 10 points in a row.

I'm well below even for the day, so I make the common and almost always deadly mistake of trying to play catch-up with some heavier bets on later games. I put $300 on Western Kentucky and $300 on Texas, and I take a $300 parlay on the two teams—and what do you know, it works. Doesn't mean it was smart, but smart and lucky don't always play on the same team. So I win $600 on the straight bets and $780 on the parlay, more than making up the deficit from the idiotic prop bets. For the day, I'm in the black.

The Bad Beat of 2008

Like most of the major casinos on the Strip, the Bellagio has a sports-betting room that looks like the love child of a Wall Street trading floor and the biggest sports bar in the universe. The main wall above the betting cage is dominated by four giant-screen TVs that would probably be visible from space, and a dozen relatively small screens, featuring nearly every NFL game and a number of thoroughbred and harness races from across the country. Everywhere you look, somebody's scoring a touchdown, some jockey's cracking the whip down the stretch . . . somebody's doing something that has the bettors clapping or yelling or moaning.

On either side of the screens, you have the Lite Brite–colored tote boards with the latest scores and point spreads, along with prop bets and odds on teams winning the Super Bowl, the World Series, the NBA Finals, and the NHL's Stanley Cup. A continuous scroll reminds us that cell phone use is strictly prohibited in the sports book—a ban that exists in every sports book in Vegas. (They don't want you on the phone with a buddy exchanging information on discrepancies in the spread from casino to casino. If you have that information, you might find an attractive "middle," a situation that occurs when there's a noticeable difference in the spread. If the Bears are four-point favorites over the Packers at the Bellagio but only one-point favorites at Caesars, you and your partner can wager a ton of dough on the Packers plus four and the Bears minus one—and if the Bears win by two or three points, you'd win both bets. At worst, you're going to break even.)

If you're betting on the races, you can take a seat in one of the cubicles with the individual TV monitors and the comfortable leather swivel chairs. Soon a waitress in a sexed-up outfit will stop by with the mantra of "Cocktails?" If you're betting on the games, you can hang at the bar or grab a spot in the seating area, which fills up quickly on game days with guys who favor replica jerseys with the names of their favorite players—or team jerseys bearing their own names. There's nothing funnier than a cigar-chomping, nachos-munching, Bud Light–swilling 40-year-old white guy from the Bronx wearing an XXL Giants jersey with Amani Toomer's name and number on his back. He's swearing up a storm, he's yelling coaching tips at the giant-screen TV, he's calling the pneumatic waitress "honey," and he's telling anyone who'll listen that he's on the roll of a lifetime.

By the time I get to the sports book, the early games have already gone off and some of the bettors are trying to make up their losses by wagering on the halftime spreads or doubling up on their late-afternoon bets.

In the long run, betting on sports is a tough, tough way to make a living. Let me rephrase that: *You can't make a living betting on sports. You will lose and lose and lose, and then you'll go broke, and then you'll lose some more, only you won't have the money to pay the bookie, so you'll lose your car, your house, your wife, your children, your dog, your job, your self-esteem, and eventually your mind. All because you think you can figure out if Citadel will beat the spread against Rutgers, or if the Browns will somehow cover against the Patriots. Stop it right now.*

I know—there are a handful of guys who are so good at finding anomalies in the point spread, so adept at picking and choosing their spots, that the sports books either impose a ceiling on the amount they can wager or ban them. (This is one of the sick things about the whole gambling industry in Vegas: if you're counting cards at the blackjack tables, which is perfectly legal, they can throw you out immediately and ban you forever. If you're really good at making sports bets, they don't have to take your action and they don't have to explain why. It's their house, their rules, too bad for you.)

A friend of mine knows more about college football than anyone this side of Lee Corso. On the second day of the NFL draft, when his beloved Green Bay Packers select some linebacker out of Boise State in the sixth round, he'll say, "That's not a bad pick. The kid's a little undersized at six-foot-one and he had that issue with his Achilles tendon his sophomore year, but he's got great football instincts, and everyone says he's matured a lot in the last year or so. He'll be a force to be reckoned with on special teams, and he could be a starter by his second year."

I know. Scary.

About once a year, my pal zeroes in on a game where he believes the spread is completely out of whack with reality. In 2008 it was Penn State–Michigan State. The teams had similar records, but even with the Nittany Lions installed as a 14-point favorite, my buddy was convinced they'd easily cover that spread. "Michigan State is soft," he said. "They've got no chance."

So on the Friday before the game, he took a morning flight from Chicago to Las Vegas, with about $25,000 in cash tucked into his jacket, his briefcase, and various pockets. (If you're traveling with more than $10,000 in cash, you're supposed to alert the authorities. My buddy isn't so keen on alerting the authorities.) He had no luggage and no hotel reservations in Las Vegas. Once he arrived at the airport, he instructed the cabbie to drop him off at the MGM Grand, where he headed straight to the sports book.

Over the next couple of hours, my pal went from sports book to sports book, betting a few grand on Penn State –14 at each stop along the way. They all took his bets, and he kept on betting until the $25,000 was gone. Then, without so much as stopping for a drink or a roll of the dice at the craps tables, my buddy got back into a cab and caught a flight back to Chicago. On Saturday afternoon, he was watching the game in his basement with his buddies, just like he does every Saturday afternoon during the college football season.

Final score: Penn State 49, Michigan State 18.

Some time over the next couple of months, my buddy then headed back to Vegas and cashed in his tickets. He wasn't tempted to make another bet; he didn't have any interest in risking a few thousand on the blackjack tables—he didn't even want to see *Mamma Mia!* at Mandalay Bay. He just headed for home and waited for the next Lock of the Year to present itself. He says he's lost a couple of those mega-bets over the years, but overall he's well above .500.

The sports books have a keen dislike for guys like my buddy, with his knowledge and his discipline and his penchant for betting big on one game instead of trying to compile a winning percentage over the course of an entire season and hundreds of games—but he's that one in a million gambler. The rest of us, we bet on too many games to ever be successful in the long run. We might ride a winning streak for a week or even a month, but eventually the juice will wear us down. I learned that the hard way when I was in my 20s. I don't bet that much on football or basketball anymore, and I almost never bet on baseball. (Anyone who bets on baseball would be better off taking a match to their cash and saving themselves the heartache. But before this month is over, I'll find myself betting more on one baseball game than I've ever risked in my life. Such is the contradictory life of the gambler, who knows one thing and often does something else.)

That said, today I'm feeling it. I grab a pencil and a couple of spreadsheets and take a gander at the latest lines. With the early games nearly over, I have three choices:

- San Francisco −7 St. Louis
- Arizona −3 Seattle
- Pittsburgh −4½ San Diego

The Cardinals are one of the surprise teams of the NFL this year, with the veteran Kurt Warner returning to MVP form at quarterback. The Seahawks are an aging, uninspired squad, and even their famously loyal fans seem to have given them up for dead. Even though I love home dogs, I'll take Arizona minus the three.

San Francisco is another team in disarray—but they're just mediocre, whereas the St. Louis Rams are so awful I'm not so sure they could beat a top-notch college team. According to a friend of mine who covers the NFL as a beat writer, the Rams are one of the worst teams of the last decade. So I'll take the 49ers and give away the seven points.

Finally, we have the Steelers against the Chargers. Pittsburgh is always tough at home, and the Chargers have been the biggest disappointment in the league thus far. A lot of experts had picked them to go to the Super Bowl, but they're under .500 and in danger of falling out of playoff contention. Factor in the weather, and I like the Steelers, even though 4½ points seems like a bit too much.

I put $1,000 on the Cardinals and another $1,000 on the 49ers. This is quite a bit more than I'd usually risk on sporting events, but I've been doing well at the blackjack tables, and besides, I'm in Vegas, where the whole idea is to do stuff you don't do back home. The Steelers-Chargers game is the marquee matchup of the late afternoon games and the one most interesting to me as a fan, so I put $1,500 on the Steelers. I also make a $1,000 parlay bet on those three teams.

Going into the fourth quarter, the Cardinals have a healthy 26–7 lead over Seattle. The Seahawks make me a squirm a bit with 13

late points, but the Cards still cover the three-point spread with a 26–20 win.

My friend the NFL beat writer was dead-on about the Rams—they're putrid. San Francisco looks like the San Francisco of the Joe Montana era, rolling to a 35–3 halftime lead and cruising to a 19-point win, easily covering the spread.

So I'm up $2,000 on my straight bets, and my three-team parlay is alive. If the Steelers cover against the Chargers, I'll net $1,500 on my straight bet on the Steelers, and $6,000 for hitting the three-team parlay.

It's snowing in Pittsburgh, and the field is muddy and slippery, hampering both offenses. A defensive struggle is never a good thing when you're giving away points. As the field conditions worsen and the players have trouble gaining their footing and hanging onto the ball, the play calling gets more conservative. Great.

The Chargers take an early 7–0 lead, but the Steelers "roar" back with a field goal and a safety in the second quarter. At halftime it's a baseball score: San Diego 7, Pittsburgh 5. With the spread, I'm actually losing 11½–5. Not hopeless. I can still take the lead with a touchdown and an extra point.

In the third quarter, the Steelers kick a field goal to go up 8–7—but with about seven minutes left in the fourth quarter, the Chargers' Nate Kaeding hits a 22-yard chip shot, and San Diego regains the lead, 10–8. I can still win this thing with a touchdown, but unless there's a defensive breakdown and I get lucky, the Steelers will be content to go for the game-winning field goal.

What makes this even more frustrating is that the Steelers have been moving the ball all day; they just can't get the damn thing into the end zone. Throughout the game, they've committed key penalties that turned touchdown drives into field-goal attempts. They were also stuffed on 4th-and-1 in the first quarter.

As the clock winds down and Ben Roethlisberger methodically leads the Steelers down the field, I know I'm screwed. Even if the Steelers get inside the 10, they'll just run it up the gut, let the clock wind down, and kick the damn field goal. They'll win the game but lose against the spread.

With 11 seconds on the clock, the field goal unit trots out, and Jeff Reed nails a chip shot from the 22 yard line. It's now Pittsburgh 11, San Diego 10—and the announcers are chirping about how this will be the first 11–10 final score in the history of the NFL. Yeah, I care about that.

I slump in my leather chair, contemplating the tickets in front of me. Fans who bet on the Chargers are already high-fiving each other and counting their winnings.

After the kickoff, there are but five ticks left on the clock—time enough for one play. San Diego has the ball on its own 21. There's not even enough time for a 50-yard bomb and a field goal attempt.

So they resort to trickery. Chargers QB Philip Rivers tosses a short pass to LaDainian Tomlinson, who laterals to wide receiver Chris Chambers, who tries to toss the ball to another teammate—but the lateral is bobbled and the ball springs loose, and all of a sudden there's a great roar in the sportsbook as Pittsburgh's Troy Polamalu picks up the ball and races untouched into the end zone as the clock runs out.

Touchdown Pittsburgh! I'm going to win the bet I had already chalked up as an *L*. Wow. Wow, wow, wow, wow, wow, wow, wow.

But hold on a minute. There's a flag on the field. No no no no no. Ah, but the flag is for an illegal forward pass by the Chargers, and of course the Steelers decline the penalty, meaning the play stands. Polamalu's teammates mob him in the end zone as the Chargers walk off the field.

In the regular football scheme of things, the final play is no big deal to anyone other than Polamalu and his family; after all, the Steelers already had the game in hand. But with the extra point, the final score is going to be Pittsburgh 18, San Diego 10—and that's a *very* big deal to everyone who has a bet on the game. Through the biggest fluke in a decade, all the losing bets just became winning bets, and vice versa.

I clutch my winning tickets in my hand and chuckle. Due to that one goofy, silly, ridiculous play, I'm looking at a *huge* swing in my favor.

The Steelers kick the extra point, the fans head for the exits, the players meet in the middle of the field to exchange handshakes, the announcers start to say goodbye. . . .

And then the referee is blowing his whistle and turning on his microphone. He's got something he wants to share with us. What could he possibly have to say? The game is over. Done. In the history books. Right?

Turns out they were reviewing the play during the extra-point attempt.

"After further review, there was no touchdown," says the ref. "After the illegal forward pass by San Diego, the ball was dead and play could not continue. The final score is Pittsburgh 11, San Diego 10."

What? What! You have got to be $#!&ing kidding me.

The TV announcers make note of this "meaningless" ruling—after all, the Steelers still won the game—and the graphics change to reflect the score.

I slump in my seat. I know there's cheering and bitching going on all over the sports book, but I don't really hear it. I'm too busy staring at my dead tickets and cursing under my breath. It's amazing how gambling directly contributes to an insanely sharp leap in foul language. In my regular life, I can go weeks if not months without uttering the word *motherfucker*. When I'm gambling, it's the equivalent of *um* or *you know*. I can't believe the motherfucking refs changed that motherfucking call. Motherfuckers.

There are no mulligans in sports betting. When the game is over, the game is over, and the refs have declared the final score is 11–10.

Later in the week, the officials will admit they made a mistake—that the play should not have been ruled dead because the ball did not hit the ground during that illegal pass, and the touchdown should have been allowed.

Great, thanks a lot. That's like your girlfriend telling you that in retrospect, she shouldn't have slept with Brad Pitt. Doesn't provide much comfort. Doesn't mean it didn't happen.

If the touchdown had been allowed, I would have won my $1,500 bet on the Steelers *plus* the three-team parlay, and I would have walked away with a tidy $9,500 profit on the three games.

Instead, I'm a winner of my two smaller bets, but I lost the bet on the Steelers and I lost the parlay even though I correctly picked two out of three games. Net result: a $550 loss. But it's hard not to think of the money I should have won, so it feels more like I lost close to 10 grand. Yeah, it would have been a miracle-fluke lucky win—but it happened, and it was *my* miracle-fluke lucky win, and I was on the right side of the gambling gods, until that bad call took it all away.

Just when you think there aren't any new ways of losing . . .

Day 4

**Bankroll:
-$70**

I'm in Las Vegas on a last-minute road trip. I had enough points on my AmEx card to cover a round-trip flight to Vegas plus hotel (travel and miscellaneous expenses are not included in my bankroll for this adventure), so at the urging of a couple of buddies who were already in Vegas and playing poker, I made some quick arrangements, threw a few things into a carry-on bag, raced up the Kennedy to O'Hare, handed my keys to the valet, hopped on the next available flight, and made it into town with just enough time to check in at my hotel and head over to a casino on the Strip where they're holding a two-week series of hold 'em tournaments. (I'm not going to mention the casino by name because of an incident that happens later in the evening, involving a young woman who may or may not be a pro, and we're not talking about poker anymore.)

Actually, they've already begun play in this tournament—but as is usually the case with events like this, you can register and join the action for at least the first couple of hours of play. (I'm thinking poker

is probably the only sport, if you want to call it a sport, where you can enter a tournament after the competition has begun. They don't let Roger Federer show up for the second round of a tennis tournament, and they don't allow those scary-smart kids to jump into the National Spelling Bee an hour after it has started, do they?) The computer-programmed monitors placed throughout the poker room reflect each new entry with an uptick in the amount of prize money available.

This is the thing about a poker tournament, as opposed to a golf championship or a tennis open: the players have to cough up their own entry fees. That's why the prize pool for the Main Event of the World Series of Poker is bigger than those of the Indy 500, the Masters, Wimbledon, and the Kentucky Derby put together. You get eight or nine thousand participants each coughing up a $10,000 entry fee, and the payouts are enormous. Now, the top-tier professional players have sponsorship deals with online sites like Full Tilt, Bodog, Ultimate Bet, and PokerStars. Breakout legends such as Phil Hellmuth also have deals with energy drinks and other sponsors. Some of these players' outfits are splattered with so many patches and labels they look like NASCAR drivers. But most players have to come up with the cash on their own.

A good number of amateur players gain entrance into major tournaments by winning "satellite" tournaments, in which they pay a few hundred bucks with the goal of finishing high enough to qualify for a buy-in to the big tournament. (In fact, as I'm writing this, I'm actually playing in a satellite tournament on the Full Tilt Poker site in a corner of the screen. It's a $216 buy-in to Full Tilt Online Poker Series Event #22, taking place later this afternoon. If I finish in the top nine among the 118 entrants in this tournament, I will win entrance to the bigger tournament, which carries a $2,620 entry fee and has a guaranteed prize pool of $2 million. On the first hand, I have 4-3 spades and I flop a straight against three players. I end up all-in against a guy who has pocket 4s and knock him out. As of this exact moment, I'm 2nd in chips . . . oops now I'm in 10th after a couple of minor losses. I was just "moved" from my virtual table to another table, with Chris

"Jesus" Ferguson taking my place. I check on Ferguson's status a few moments later. He's out of the satellite in 98th place. Imagine that—I just finished higher in a tournament than one of the greatest players in the history of the game.) But one way or another, every player in a tournament fills out a form and hands over the entry fee. The tournament hosts take their cut, and the rest goes into the prize pool.

For a medium-large tourney, the prize structure usually pays out about 27 percent for first place, 17 percent for second, 12 percent for third, 8 percent for fourth, and down the line, with about 10 percent of the players cashing. The structure varies according to the size of the tournament. And though they never talk about this on TV, when it gets down to the final few players, side deals are often struck in which players agree to "chop," or split, the prize pool based on how many chips everyone has at the time. The online sites are more upfront about this and even have specific rules about chopping in their major tournaments—e.g., the PokerStars Sunday Million, which states, "Any deal at the final table must leave at least $30,000 aside for the tournament champion."

This tourney is a no limit hold 'em event with a $1,560 buy-in. There are approximately two hundred players at about 25 tables that have been set up outside the casino's poker room, which isn't large enough to accommodate this much action while continuing to cater to the smaller tournaments and the cash-game action.

As I make my way to my table, I see a couple of familiar faces from Chicago: Jeff and Rocco. I know these guys only by first name and face. Like about a million other young men in their 20s, they're poker players who just might be good enough to turn pro—and the only way to find out is by playing in tournaments and cash games all over the country while they're still callow enough and fearless enough to take such chances. Jeff's in this tournament; Rocco has made the final table of a tournament that started yesterday and will conclude today. They know about this book and they tell me they've got a million stories for me. We exchange contact information. I never hear from them again. Maybe they don't want to be in the book. Yes, poker has

become a mainstream staple on ESPN. Yes, poker rooms are popping up in casinos all over the United States. Nevertheless, there's still a stigma attached to the lifestyle.

I take my assigned seat and receive $10,000 in chips. (These chips have no value outside the world of this particular tournament. When you watch poker on TV and you see dollar amounts attached to chips, that's just a way of keeping score.) My best move at the outset is to play conservatively, especially because these players have already been at it for an hour or so and they know a little bit about each other's tendencies, whereas I know nothing about them. I don't know who's aggressive, who's passive, who's crazy, who has no idea what they're doing and shouldn't even be in a tournament of this caliber. It's one of the oldest cliches in poker—you don't play the cards, you play the players.

That said, if you never get good cards, you're not going to win. Early on, I get some nice hands and some even nicer flops. Queen-Jack suited in my hand turns into a straight, and a guy with two pair calls me all the way. With A-Q, I get the nut straight, again taking chips from the same guy, who once again has two pair and is glaring at me from behind his sunglasses now. "Guess we have a new luckbox at the table," he says with a thin smile.

"How about that President Obama?" I reply. "I really think he's going to turn this economy around."

I try not to get involved in much trash talk at the table, as I find it to be one of the most unappealing aspects of the 21st-century poker experience. Whether it's in person or online, there's a whole breed of poker players who believe it's perfectly acceptable to insult, tease, prod, or otherwise taunt your opponents, all in the name of games-manship. I enjoy a little verbal sparring, and I'm always up for some levity when the moment calls for it, but I don't buy into the nasty stuff or the personal insults. I don't believe you can berate somebody at the table and then walk away and say, "That's just my poker persona. It's nothing personal." I've met Phil Hellmuth, the all-time bracelet winner at the World Series of Poker, on a number of occasions. We've exchanged correspondence. He once sent me a box of signed items, and I returned the favor by sending him and his wife a box of some my favorite movies on DVD. He seems like a great guy. That said, some of his televised antics over the years, while undeniably entertaining, are embarrassing for a grown man.

All-time bracelet winner Phil Hellmuth interviews me after a tournament. In the background is Andy Bloch, an original member of the infamous MIT blackjack team.

(NOTE: As I write this, I am no longer playing in that online tournament; I was eliminated in 28th place. That means I finished in the top 30 percent, but it's no better than being the first one to get knocked out, as only the top 9 will advance to the big-ass tournament. After my early flourish, I couldn't catch shit and I simply ran out of chips. Frustrating.)

I get Ace-Queen but the flop misses me. I play 6-5 suited and nothing good comes of it. When my Ace-King hits top pair and I make a big bet, only to get raised an insane amount by a talky Greek, I fold the hand and commit myself to an ultraconservative round or two so I can observe my opponents.

The Greek, who's about 65, won't shut up. He talks to the dealer; he talks to the waitresses; he talks on his cell phone. (You have to step away from the table if you want to text or make phone calls. The rule is in place to deter collusion among players.) Sitting to his left is a French-Canadian woman of a certain age. She is dripping with jewelry and she is wearing oversized Chanel sunglasses, and she has a relentless style of play more befitting one of those maniacal 20-something Euro-players than someone who looks like she should be going over page proofs for *Vogue*.

To my left is a graduate student of Italian-Persian heritage from the San Diego area. (He tells me this when we chat during a break.

His father, the Italian, has encouraged him to enjoy his time at the poker table as he considers taking a year off from his math studies to go on the tournament circuit. His Persian mother is horrified at the idea.) Also at the table: the obligatory collection of white guys in baseball caps, T-shirts, big watches, and sunglasses. They're all pretty solid players and most likely they've all watched entirely too much poker on TV and have big dreams of becoming the next instant millionaire.

I started with $10,000 in chips. I now have about $13,000 and I'm feeling pretty good about things. But consider that in order to win any tournament, you have to accumulate *everyone's* chips. There are 1.98 million chips in play right now. All of a sudden, 13,000 chips seem like a ridiculous pittance.

For the next couple of hours, I hold steady as players around me are eliminated while others start racking up some impressive chip counts. I'm just somewhere in the middle of the pack. I limp in (meaning I don't raise the pot, I just call the amount of the big blind) with an A-10, and there are four players seeing a flop.

It comes A-10-8 rainbow, giving me top two pair, a very strong hand. I bet accordingly. Two players fold, but the French-Canadian woman calls.

The turn is a 4. I bet again—a big bet, nearly the size of the pot. She calls.

The river comes: a 9. I bet again—and she goes all-in.

What could she have? It's possible she flopped a set of 8s, or she made a bad call with 9-9 on the flop and the turn and got lucky on the river. There's a straight out there, but only if she is holding 7-6 or J-7 or Q-J. I suppose it's possible she has a Q-J and she made the call after the flop because she had eight chances at a straight. That's not a very good play, but at least it's within the realm of possibility. Only an idiot would have stuck around until the river with a 7-6 or a J-7, hoping for a 9 that would give you a straight but wouldn't necessarily guarantee a win. It would be an incredibly dumb play.

I've got her covered, meaning I have more chips than she does, so I can call her all-in bet without getting knocked out of the tournament. The odds say I should make the call. My instincts tell me that even though this woman has been playing like a maniac, the all-in bet doesn't make sense as a bluff because I'm "pot committed" due to the amount of chips I've already released to the pot. But I really don't have any choice. I call with my top two pair.

She turns over the J-7. Yep, she has a straight. Yep, she should have folded before the turn, after the turn, and after the flop.

After the flop, I was an 82 percent favorite.

After the turn, I was a 90 percent favorite.

After the river, I was dead.

She got one of the four cards in the deck that put her ahead of me. As she rakes in her chips, shaking her head and saying, "I had a feeling," the kid next to me gives me a look that says, "Ouch," while the Greek says, "How could you stay in with that hand!" to the woman. She just repeats her comment: "I had a feeling."

Yeah, I have a feeling, too. I'm about to get sick.

On the very next hand, I call a raise with A-8 of hearts and I flop a flush. My friend from San Diego bets and I raise. He calls. On the turn he checks and I bet. He calls. Same pattern on the river. Turns out he had flopped a set of Jacks, but the board didn't pair so my flush held up. I get a little healthier, but I still don't have as much as I did before the disastrous hand against the Premier of Quebec.

We're down to 137 players.

The player to my immediate right is eliminated. His seat is taken by a DiCaprio-looking guy in an oversized trucker cap, Bose headphones, a North Carolina basketball jersey, sunglasses. He looks like a caricature of the aggressive young poker player—and he plays like one as well. Raising every pot, never changing expressions, taking off his headphones only when one of his buddies happens by the table to talk smack. He and his friends have a "last longer" pool going. Whoever goes furthest in this tournament among their group will get two grand.

He raises my big blind twice. The first time I fold. The second time I call with 9-7, a garbage hand. When an Ace comes on the flop and I bet, he folds. I show him the 9-7 bluff. He doesn't react. That was fun.

Later, we get into a betting war, and I'm bluffing all the way. He calls me down, and I'm sure I'm beat—but it turns out we have the same hand. Maybe I shouldn't have shown him that 9-7.

I make a standard raise with Ace-Queen and my nemesis from Canada calls. Flop comes A-J-4; turn and river are irrelevant. Sure enough, she has Ace-Jack and takes the pot from me.

It's late afternoon now, and a few players are switching from coffee drinks and Red Bulls to Bloody Marys or beers. I've learned from experience that if you're going to play in a tournament that can go for 10 or 12 hours, there's little brilliance in starting to drink adult beverages in the fourth or fifth hour of play. I stick with my coffee.

If you want a massage while you're playing, no problem. Young women patrol the tournament area, offering back and neck rubs for a fee. Guys flip their seats around and lean over the table, continuing to play their hands while getting a rubdown. (I suppose the female players could ask for a massage as well, but I've never seen that, nor can I recall seeing male massage dudes offering their services. Discrimination!)

Male dealers often make comments about attractive women who pass by the tournament area. Male players often chime in with comments of their own. These remarks are almost never creative or particularly enlightened.

We've been playing for six hours, and the field has been cut in half. There are 99 players left. Another 100 or so have moved on with their lives. They're playing in a cash game or drinking or shopping or napping or arguing with their significant other, who didn't think they were going to play *that* much poker on this vacation. Whatever they're doing, they're out and I'm still in the game, and there's always a bit of a giddy feeling when you're still alive and the tournament has been going on for a while. You start thinking/dreaming, *I might just win this thing.*

On the last hand before the dinner break, I get a pair of Queens in the big blind. A young Asian player raises me, and I pretend to deliberate for a while before going all-in.

He thinks for a long time. A long, long, long time. At this point I know I have the better hand, because the only two hands that beat me are A-A and K-K, and if he had either one of those hands he would have insta-called. So he has something like A-K or A-Q, or a smaller pair than mine. Finally he calls—and sure enough, he has a pair of 10s.

I am a 4-1 favorite. Barring a particularly unusual sequence of cards, his best chance to beat me is by catching one of the two remaining 10s in the deck. That doesn't happen, and I rake in a healthy pot that gives me more chips than I've had at any point in the tournament. I'm back!

For about two hours, I pick up mediocre hand after mediocre hand, as the blinds go up and my chip stack slowly dwindles. I try to make a few moves by raising with hands like K-10 and 9-8 suited—but usually I get called or raised, or I have to abandon the hand after the flop. There are 88 players left, and I'm probably about 60th.

With A-9, I go all-in. The big blind wakes up with A-K and makes an easy call—but I get lucky on the flop with a 9 to take the lead. On the turn, he picks up a flush draw, and sure enough, he completes the runner-runner* to get the flush and knock me out. I can't complain much, seeing as how he was a heavy favorite before we turned the cards, but there's still that moment of dread when you see the last card and you're saying "No spade, no spade, no spade, no spade!" and of course it comes up a spade.

---

* A "runner-runner" is when a player gets the two cards he needs to make a hand on the turn and the river, respectively. It usually means that player has "sucked out"—i.e. come from behind to pull off a miracle upset.

I'm out, finishing about 70th, which means nothing in terms of cash return. Sure, I picked up some more tournament experience, and I outlasted about two-thirds of the field, but I was still a long way from reaching the money.

I shake hands with a few players, gather my stuff, check in with a friend who's still alive in the tournament—and then I take the walk of shame out of the tournament area, replaying hands in my head and muttering under my breath as I blend in with the other gamblers and tourists in the casino. Another tournament, another respectable showing—another disappointment.

I've got bets in the NCAA tournament on Syracuse, Xavier, Kansas, Cleveland State, Marquette, Michigan State, Sienna, and Pittsburgh, along with a few over/under picks and some parlays. And seeing as how I'm at a casino, how can I not play a little blackjack and roll some dice?

All of a sudden it's 3 A.M. and I'm sitting with a couple of my buddies. (One was knocked out in the first hour of the poker tournament. The other finished 22nd.) Karl is taking me through the paces of three-card poker, one of the more popular new table games. You walk through the blackjack area these days and you realize half the tables aren't offering good ol' regular blackjack—they're offering pai gow poker, three-card poker, Let It Ride, Blackjack Switch, and other wacky games.

For three-card poker, there are three betting circles on the felt, and you get dealt three cards. (That's why they call it three-card poker instead of, say, four-card poker.) The rankings are different than for five-card poker. For one thing, you can't get a full house. A straight flush is best, followed by three of a kind, a straight (in this game, 6-7-8 is a straight), a flush, and a pair. At one point during the action you have the option to fold, and I'm told you should fold if you have a hand worse than Q-6-4. Quite frankly, it seems like kind of a stupid game.

We've had a drink. Maybe two. Maybe five. But we're in fine shape compared to the woman who looks like a well-fed Amy Winehouse as she staggers up and squeezes into the seat between my two friends and me. (Three guys will never sit on three consecutive chairs if there's an empty chair available, just as they'd never stand three across at the urinals if there are four or more available.)

"Whatcha playing?" she says as she plunks her purple leather bag on the table, immediately drawing the attention of the pit boss, who comes over and tells her she can't put her purse on the table.

She asks me if I'll give her $100 in chips so she can play. I decline. The pit boss tells her she's going to have to get up if she doesn't play, so she reluctantly pulls out a stack of red and green chips, and if she had those chips, hmm, why did she ask *me* for some? Being the observational genius that I am, it occurs to me she just might be a professional escort of some kind—although it's hardly professional for her to be this sloshed if she's on the job, so to speak.

A word here about hookers and strippers—and, yes, I know there's sometimes a great difference between the two and sometimes no difference at all. I've been to strip clubs and I've written a few columns about strippers. About 15 years ago, I met and became friends with a woman who eventually let me know she took off her clothes for a living. She was Stripper Stereotype #3: the bright girl with a tough upbringing who had a child when she was 17 and was determined to quit the business as soon as she had saved up enough money to go back to school.

On a couple of occasions, I've gone to strip clubs with a female companion who was curious to see what the experience was all about. But I've never gone to a strip club by myself or with a bunch of buddies. I've never had any interest in hanging out in some dark, depressing place where Lady Gaga and the Pussycat Dolls are booming on the sound system while dead-eyed women with fake breasts undulate in various states of undress. I don't have some rescue fantasy about strippers. I don't want some woman to dance in the vicinity of my lap as long as I keep shoveling twenties her way. It's just not my thing.

Maybe it's ego or whatever, but I have no interest in a woman who has to be paid to feign interest in me.

Nor can I imagine a scenario in which I'd be interested in spending any intimate time with a hooker. I'm Journalist Stereotype #27: the guy who would rather interview the hooker and find out how she got to this place than sleep with her in a cash exchange.

I remember getting on an elevator in a casino in Vegas about 10 to 12 years ago and hearing, "Can you hold the door?" In stepped two of the most stunning women I'd ever seen in my life. They were as gorgeous as the starlets I see on the red carpet at the Oscars.

As the elevator raced up to the high floors and the women primped a bit, one said to the other, "So what are these guys' names again?"

Her friend replied, "Um, Jack and . . . I don't know. I can't remember the other guy's name. Melanie knows the one guy from his last time out—she says he's really nice and *really* rich."

Apparently they weren't on their way up to meet their longtime boyfriends.

Without knowing anything about either of those women, I might have been too intimidated to even ask one for a date. In our superficial world, you'd think either one of those gals could have married a millionaire within a week if they so desired. That's just on looks alone—and for all I know they were both sophisticated conversationalists and dedicated humanitarians as well. Yet there they were in that elevator, trying to remember the names of the men with whom they would soon be trysting. For money.

A dozen years later, those women from the elevator are in their mid-30s, I would imagine. You wonder if they're still working and living in Vegas, or living entirely different lives, a thousand miles and a hundred dark memories removed from that elevator.

In the meantime, the 20ish-looking woman sitting next to me, who's pretty but not beautiful, who is wearing too much makeup, who doesn't really have the legs for that micro-miniskirt—she loses her money and she gulps down the rest of her drink, and she turns and winks at me as she leans back, her chair tilting . . .

And she falls flat on the floor, her legs up in the air as her chair crashes next to her.

She is not hurt. She cries, "Fuck!"

I reach down and pick up the chair as I extend my hand to the woman. (I have to admit I reached for the chair first. But just barely and just to make sure nobody tripped over it.) She ignores me and starts laughing.

The pit boss comes over as the young woman struggles to her feet, still laughing and cursing. He tells her it's time to go home.

She takes one more stab at my friends and me, asking if we'd like to meet her at the bar. We pass.

Our dealer shakes his head. The pit boss apologizes for the disruption.

We go back to the stupid three-card poker game. I lose a couple of hundred bucks and announce that it's time for me to bid farewell. Gotta get ready to fly back to Chicago tomorrow. More gambling awaits. As I walk past the bar, I see the Amy Winehouse–looking young woman engaged in conversation with two beefy guys. She seems to have regained her composure a bit. Maybe she'll make some money tonight after all.

The Odds

The house edge is the casino's built-in advantage. If you're playing roulette and your number hits, you get paid off at 36-1. At first that seems like a straight-up fair deal, considering the highest number you can select is 36.

Ah, but what about "0" and "00"? In fact there are *38* possible numbers you can select, but if you win you don't get paid off at 38-1. That difference gives the house an edge of 5.26 percent. The longer you play, the more likely it is the house edge will wear you

down. And the more exotic the bets—for example, betting on the hard 4 in craps—the bigger the odds against you.

Percentages will vary slightly from casino to casino, but here's the average house edge in the most popular casino games. In games where the player has to make decisions, the percentages are based on the player making the correct play (e.g., never splitting 10s or hitting on 17 in blackjack.)

Game	House Edge
Baccarat (if you bet on Banker)	1.17%
Baccarat (if you bet on Player)	1.36%
Baccarat (if you bet on Tie)	14.1%
Big Six	20%
Blackjack (multiple decks)	0.63%
Caribbean Stud Poker	5.2%
Craps (Pass/Come only)	1.4%
Craps (Pass + 10x odds)	0.02%
Craps (Any craps)	11.1%
Craps (Big 6 or Big 8)	9.1%
Craps (Hard 4 or Hard 10)	11.1%
Keno	29%
Let It Ride	3.5%
Pai Gow Poker	2.5%
Roulette	5.26%
Slots (nickel)	15%
Slots (dollar)	8%
Slots ($100)	3.9%
Video Poker	5%
Video Poker, if played perfectly at high stakes	Essentially even

So if you played by-the-book blackjack, bet only Pass/Come and took the odds in craps, or played perfect video poker, the house edge would be less than 1 percent. If you've got the stamina, the bankroll, and the knowledge, most of your trips to Vegas or your neighborhood casino will be relatively painless.

But if you're playing the slots and keno, if you're spreading chips all over the craps table, if you like to bet on Tie at the baccarat table, either you don't care about losing your money or you're under some mad delusion that these games can be beaten. They can't.

Day 5

**Bankroll:
-$1,630**

After the opening weekend of the NCAA tournament, I am leading in a couple of office pools—and I am 54th in the country in the CBSSports.com pool, which has more than two million entries. That's crazy lucky. It's too bad it won't matter if I finish 1st, 54th, or 9,999th in that CBS pool, as the top 10,000 will all be thrown into a virtual hat and one name will be chosen at random. Remember, this is a *sweepstakes*.

Gambling is in the news all the time. All the time.

Headline: "Facebook Coming Under Scrutiny for Online Gambling."

Headline: "Online Pools: Pastime or Crime? Wild Popularity on Networking Sites Raises New Legal Issues."

Headline: "NBA Star Iverson Banned from Two Detroit Casinos."

Headline: "Casinos Deny Iverson Was Banned."

Headline: "Delaware Gambling Expansion Threatens Maryland Slots Revenue."

Headline: "Delaware Legalizes Sports Gambling."

Headline: "Gambling and Education Go Hand in Hand for Teri Hatcher."

According to that last story, the *Desperate Housewives* actress is quoted as saying, "I do use the opportunity to make [Hatcher's daughter] understand math and what you're betting and what you get back . . . so we work on math. It's fun."

Our love/hate, legal/illegal relationship with gambling is reflected in the news. In Webb County, Texas, tax assessor Patricia Barrera is booked on gambling charges. But in Delaware, they're legalizing sports betting. In Baltimore, they're lamenting the dropoff in revenue from horse racing. But in Pennsylvania, a church is leading a crusade against gambling. In a small town in Massachusetts, residents have approved a casino project. In Ohio, a new poll shows that 60 percent of residents favor legalized gambling.

Another headline I came across while working on the book:

"Elgin Man Sentenced to 4 Years on Gambling Conviction."

The *Chicago Tribune* reports that a "man who has already served three prison stints for gambling convictions [has been] sentenced to a 4-year prison term for running high-stakes at two taverns in Kane County . . . Authorities said [Michael] Alvarez operated Super Bowl betting pools in 2007. One of the pools featured 100 squares, with bettors paying $600 per square."

In the meantime, the Illinois State Lottery is offering all kinds of games that are no different than Super Bowl square pools. Games where you pick numbers or you scratch off squares and you hope to get lucky. The Illinois State Lottery drawing is televised on WGN-TV every night, but a guy running a Super Bowl pool in a tavern owned by his wife—he's a hardcore criminal. He needs to be put away.

Look, I'm not saying a three-time loser who continues to operate an illegal gambling pool is a genius or a saint. But in a sane world, he wouldn't be breaking the law by running a high-stakes Super Bowl pool.

I don't believe most state and federal lawmakers actually see fundamental moral differences between, say, playing the lottery and betting on the Bears to cover the spread against the Packers. It's hard to argue that spending a day at the track or playing craps in a state-sanctioned casino is somehow a more productive use of one's time than playing in an illegal, high-stakes cash poker game at someone's house or calling a bookmaker and placing a bet. It's all about gauging public perception—not so much the value system of those of us who gamble all the time, but the populace at large. Horse racing is an established sport with a rich tradition. Casinos, in addition to gaming tables, have steak restaurants and concert venues and souvenir shops. The lottery is a fun fantasy game, with smiling blondes announcing the winning numbers on TV. The average nongambler may have no interest in these endeavors, but he or she is hardly going to vote against a state rep because the politico is in favor of using lottery funds and horse racing revenue to supplement the state's education fund.

Lawmakers are nothing if not flexible. If they sense a shift in the public perception of a certain type of gambling—say, video poker machines in bars—some of them will act accordingly and push to legalize or criminalize those activities. The government's seemingly inconsistent attitude about gambling is much akin to its take on mind-altering substances. Even though one might argue that the occasional toke on a joint is less harmful than guzzling six tumblers of Scotch every night, your state senator or congressman wouldn't think of trying to bring back Prohibition, nor would he or she make the decriminalization of marijuana a key campaign issue. Why? Because the typical voter still thinks pot is a dangerous gateway drug, whereas there's nothing wrong with the occasional drink.

Before getting on the plane and heading back to Chicago, I play some blackjack, starting at $50 a hand and working up to $100 and then $200 per wager. My blackjack strategy has always been pretty consistent, regardless of the stakes. Probably 95 percent of my plays are strictly by the book—always hit on 16 if the dealer shows a 7 or higher, always stand if I've got higher than 11 and the dealer is showing a "bust card" such as a 4 or a 5, never split 10s or face cards, always split Aces, etc.

There's a scene in *The Gambler* in which James Caan hits on a hard 18. The dealer tries to talk him out of it, but Caan says quietly, "Give me the 3."

He gets the 3.

I've always wanted to duplicate that scene in a casino, but a) I'll probably get a 10 and everyone at the table will throw their drinks at me, or b) I'll get the 3 and security will be at my table two minutes later, inviting me to take my business elsewhere.

Occasionally, if I feel I have a sense of the deck or I'm in the mood to gamble, I'll take a hit when the book says I should stand, or I'll double down on a marginally superior hand, or I'll engage in some unorthodox betting pattern—e.g., starting with a $50 wager and continuing to double the wager until I lose or I reach $800, whichever comes first. There are dozens of systems "guaranteed" to beat the game—but you can't beat the odds of the game any more than you can bend mathematics so that 2 + 2 = anything other than 4. You can minimize your disadvantage to the point where you have a fighting chance, but if anyone tries to sell you a revolutionary method of winning at blackjack, here's the question I would ask: "Why are you willing to sell that system to me for $39.95 when you could be utilizing it to win $10 million?"

As for insurance—i.e., the dealer shows an Ace and you can bet half your original wager that he or she has a 10-card underneath—at a very advanced level of play, card counters can find situations where it makes sense to take insurance. But for you and for me, it is almost never a smart move. The house edge on insurance is about 7 percent. Plus, taking insurance fosters negativity! You have to believe the dealer isn't going to turn over that 21 when he's showing an Ace.

Most blackjack dealers will be happy to tell you what "the book" says if you're confused about a hand. They might not flat-out say, "You should split those 9s against my 5 card," but they might say something like, "The book says you should split 'em, but it's up to you."

I never offer advice at the blackjack table unless I'm asked. For one thing, I'm no expert. Nor do I believe in the theory that says if the guy in front of you makes the wrong play, it screws up your hand. This concept is very difficult for even some knowledgeable players to grasp—the play of others *doesn't affect you in the long run.* Mathematically, your odds remain the same. Granted, if someone constantly makes bad decisions at your table, it's likely to wear on you from a psychological perspective and you're better off leaving the table. But for every time someone hits when he or she shouldn't hit and you wind up with a card that busts your hand, someone else will make a mistake that benefits you.

Now, if someone asks me, "What do you think I should do?" my first answer is always: "It's your money—you should play the hand however you see fit." But then I'll follow it up with, "I'd double down with that A-7 against her 5. You can't bust, and the value of your hand isn't nearly as important here as the fact that she's got a card that could very well result in her busting." I've seen players berate strangers at the table for making unorthodox plays. Hey, if you don't like it, move to another table or play one-on-one with a dealer or against a machine.

As for money management: I'm a firm believer in walking away when you're getting killed. I don't always practice this belief, but then again, I'm a Catholic and I'm not always first in line for Sunday mass either. If you put $1,000 out there and you bleed off all your chips, reaching into your pocket for another grand rarely gets you back to even. Better to walk away, take a breather.

When I'm on a roll, I will increase the amount of my wager and I'll try to turn the solid session into something special. But I cringe when

someone is up a few grand and they start making wild plays with the time-honored rationalization of "I'm playing with the house's money."

No! You're playing with *your* money. The moment the dealer slides that chip over to you after a winning hand is the moment that money is yours. When you get paid at work, are you spending the company's money? Heck no. You should treat your profits with the same respect you treat the money you brought to Vegas. The problem with those damn chips is they never feel like real money. If you're up five grand and they hand you a single "chocolate chip" with "$5,000" imprinted on it, that's just not the same as having a wad of $100 bills. Your best move when you're up a bunch is to take some of those chips to the cashier and exchange them for cold hard cash.

(Now, in a cash poker game, it's considered an egregious offense to take chips off the table and pocket them in the middle of a game. The term for it is "going south." On the show *High Stakes Poker* on the Game Show Network a few seasons ago, poker pro Freddy Deeb was deeply insulted when a couple of players half-jokingly insinuated he had gone south while taking a five-minute break from the game. Deeb wouldn't let it go until he had received an apology from all concerned. You would have thought someone had insulted his mother. But that unwritten rule doesn't apply to blackjack. It's your money. You can do whatever you want with it.)

At one point in this session I get 8-8 and I split 'em, per the book, and I get another 8—so now I've got three $200 bets out there, and I double down on one bet and I get 21, and the other two are 18s, and the dealer busts—and that's a net profit of $800. On that note, time to get out of town.

As I make my way through the airport, I flash back to one of my first trips to Las Vegas, shortly after my 21st birthday, when I had a hand similar to the one described above. . . .

You're at the blackjack table in Las Vegas on the third day of a three-day vacation. It's your first gambling trip to Vegas—and your last night before you return to snowy Chicago and real life.

You're playing your favorite game, and the cards are going your way.

You started with a stack of the red $5 chips. Twenty of them to begin: you'd put five twenties on the felt, just like the how-to books said you should do it, and felt your heart skip a beat when the dealer counted out the money and gave you those chips along with the obligatory "Good luck, sir."

After an hour, the stack has started to grow. You've hit at least three blackjacks, you keep 19s and 20s—and when you're stuck with a junk hand like 15 or 16, more often that not it's the dealer that busts.

This game is easy! Just like when you're playing at home in somebody's basement—when you're getting the cards, you're getting the cards. You're up at least $300, maybe $350. That's more than you make in a week. You're starting to fantasize about reaching the $1,000 in mark in profits and walking away. Or maybe you'll walk away when you reach $1,500 or $2,000 in profits. Why stop when you're on a roll?

Another free light beer from the waitress with the blue eye shadow and the tip-me-please cleavage? Why not! You're feeling a bit light-headed, but you're not even close to drunk. It's more like you're wired from the success you're having at the table. You cannot wait to tell this story to your girlfriend back home.

This is why people come to Vegas: that moment when you're on a roll and you actually believe you can will the cards to come your way. The moment when you feel like James Bond. At this moment, you're not a bank executive from Cincinnati or a commodities trader from Philly or an attorney from Phoenix—or some kid from Chicago with a bad haircut who shouldn't even be at this table, given that you've got more bills than cash in your life at this point. Doesn't matter. You're a ramblin', gamblin' man.

After another ministreak, the dealer "colors up" some of your chips, turning some of the $5 reds into a smaller stack of $25 greens and even

a few black $100 chips. (They always make it sound like they're doing it as a favor, to make your stack more manageable, when the truth is that four green $25 chips or a single $100 chip seem even less like real money than 20 of the red $5 chips. The better to wager with!)

*After a couple of hours, you're up nearly $500. **Five hondo**, baby. For the last half hour, you've been betting two $25 chips per hand—but now you're really feeling it, and yeah, maybe you're more than a little buzzed, so you place three black $100 chips in the circle in front of you.*

Deep breath.

You watch as the long-nailed dealer with the tough-to-pronounce name and the stoic expression reaches for the cards and begins to distribute them with the speed of a magician working the midnight show at the Trop. At that moment, you can barely hear the Fleetwood Mac cover band playing at the bar behind you; you don't really hear the chiming of the slots or the chatter of your fellow players. It's all about this moment, this hand, this impending victory.

Your first card is a big fat ugly 6. Brutal.

But then comes a glorious 5—glorious for this situation, that is—giving you an 11, with all its potential and promise. (Years later, you'll hear someone describe the 11 as the Mary-Kate Olsen of blackjack hands—you just know it'll be something when it hits 21. You'll think about notifying the authorities, because anyone who thinks that way just might be in a certain kind of database somewhere.)

Long Nails shows a 9, meaning she most likely has 19, so if you get a 10 or a face card, you'll have 21 and you'll be winner.

You know what to do. You know what must be done. If you're not going to double down in this spot, with the odds in your favor and the stakes higher than they've been all night—well, you might just as well slink off to the quarter slots and join the rest of the timid amateurs who come all the way to Vegas only to spend the entire time slumped in front of a machine, touching buttons and muttering about the cocktail waitress who seems to have forgotten about them.

Fingers trembling ever so slightly, you place three black chips behind the original stack and say, "Double down." (Why does your voice sound like Anthony Michael Hall's in a John Hughes teen comedy?) Now you're risking $600—everything you've won, and some of your own money as well—on a single hand.

In that split second before the next card comes your way, you feel a mixture of excitement, anxiety, naked fear, and pure adrenaline.

Also, you feel kind of stupid. **What the hell am I doing?**

Especially because your entire bankroll for the trip was $250, and you have about $14.50 in total assets waiting for you at home, including the 1976 Camaro with 104,540 miles on it. You'd have to work two full weeks to bring home $600, and by the time you got that paycheck, about $540 would already be designated to paying bills.

So $600, yeah, that's pretty much a friggin' fortune at this point in your life.

She's supposed to give you a Queen or a Jack or a King or a 10 so you'll get 21. And then she'll turn over her 19, and she'll match your $600 chips with six black chips from the dealer's tray.

But she doesn't give you a 10. She drops a five in your lap, giving you a horrible 16. And you can't even take the chance and hit on the 16, because when you double down you get just one card and one card only.

You're probably dead—but maybe, just maybe, she'll have a six underneath that nine, giving her a 15 and forcing her to hit. She could bust and you'd still win. It happens.

She turns over her card. It's not a 10. She doesn't have a 19.

It's an Ace. She has 20. She says it in a low voice with no expression, "Twenty," she says, and she scoops up your cards and your two stacks of black chips with about as much emotion as a waitress would show if she were wiping a ring of water from a Formica counter top. Some dealers pretend to care when you lose. Some might care for real. This one doesn't give a shit.

You're done. You keep playing, but you're done. Seems like every time you have 19, she has 20. When you hit on 13, you bust. When she hits on 14, she gets 21.

By the time you stagger off your stool, your pockets are virtually empty. You're still in Vegas but you'd give anything to be back home,

because you don't have any money, and there's no worse place in the world to be broke than in Vegas.

That was Saturday night. Your buddy picked up the tab for a few more drinks and lent you a few dollars to get you through the next day. He has a flight back to L.A. early Sunday morning—but you're stuck in town until about 10 P.M. Vegas time. You wait as long as possible to check out, and then you kick around town for several hours before finally heading to the airport. By the time you pay your cabbie and salt away the money you'll need to get from Midway Airport to your home, you have about 10 bucks and change in your pocket. You get a beer for three bucks and nurse it while watching sports highlights in the bar. Before ordering another one, you figure you should check on your flight.

Delayed. Snow in Chicago.

You might well be spending the night in the airport. (You sure as hell don't have the funds to get a hotel room.) No point in getting one more beer. No point in eating. You're not hungry.

You wander into a bookstore and search the paperback racks and find a book called Desert Rose, *by Larry McMurtry, one of the great American authors of the century. It is the story of a Vegas showgirl and her rebellious daughter. You read it not so long ago in the library back home—there was a time in your life when you spent many hours hiding in the bowels of libraries, reading novels all the way through and avoiding certain things and certain people—but you're going to read it again, because you could use the comfort of a good read. It's almost as good as running into an old friend in this damn airport, with its jangling slot machines and its oversized advertisements for magicians and pop singers.*

For the next couple of hours, the sounds of the airport seem to fade to nothingness. It's like the moment of the bet, when you don't hear anything and you don't care about anything but the next card. You escape again, this time into the world of a showgirl named Rose. The story is so good it's almost enough to make you forget about your disaster of a trip out here. It's almost enough to remind you that every day you spend gambling is a day you spend away from your ambitions to write and to talk on the radio for a living.

Almost.

Day 6

Bankroll:
+$70

"America now has twice as many publicly available gaming devices that take money—slot and video poker machines and electronic lottery outlets—than it does ATMs that dispense it."
—*Atlantic Monthly*, December 2005

Over five days of gambling, I have placed tens of thousands of dollars in bets.

And I'm up a grand total of $70.

One way to look at that would be to say I'm hanging tough. All that time at the poker tables, all those sports wagers, the fatal battles with the Bodog blackjack beast—and yet I have my head, or at least one hair on my head, above water. Good show!

I think I'll go with that option. It's better than saying I feel like I've gone five rounds in the ring with Chuck Liddell, I'm just barely standing—and I've got 25 rounds to go.

What better time to tackle the most popular casino game of all?

Walk onto virtually any casino floor in America, and the first game of chance you're going to encounter is the slots. Row after row of brightly-colored, gleaming, humming, singing, talking slot machines, offering you the chance to step right up and win $14,984, or $26,398, or $37,542—the numbers increasing before your very eyes as patrons keep pushing those buttons and inserting their vouchers and bills into the ever-hungry mouths of the machines.

You'll have to navigate past the slots to get to the craps tables, the blackjack tables, the sports book, and the poker room. At times it seems as if the slot machines have the other games surrounded. They dominate. Why? Because the slots remain the most popular game among gamblers—and the slots are the biggest money-maker for the casinos. (In a nod to the poker boom of the 21st century, many casinos have in recent years built new poker rooms or expanded their existing areas, but they almost always have these relatively small rooms tucked into a far corner of the floor, next to the sports book. They'll take their rake from the cash games, and they'll charge a fee to all tournament players—but it's nowhere near the kind of money that can be made by adding another few hundred slot machines to the mix.)

Next time you're in a casino, take a good look at the layout and you'll see the slots occupy as much floor space as probably every other game put together. You might have to walk around a bit to find an opening at a craps table or an empty seat at the blackjack table. There might be a waiting list for the cash games in the poker room. But there's always an opening at a slot machine, because there are thousands of such machines in most major casinos. Statistics vary, but the best bet is that casinos make about 70 percent of their profits from the slot machines. (They call it the "one-armed bandit," not the "one-armed charity center.")

For a long time, slots were there mainly to give the casual gambler—or the gambler's significant other—something to do. Bugsy Siegel installed slots in the Flamingo so the wives and the girlfriends of the high rollers could keep themselves occupied while the men rolled the dice and played cards. The slots were not for men or for serious players. The machines were well-crafted, attractive devices, but not all that fascinating or mesmerizing. Mechanical reels, a lever on the right side of the machine (another example of discrimination against lefties), a slot for you to insert coins, a bin for the coins to land if you hit a winner. Fairly simple.

These days, some slot banks look more complicated and have more bells and whistles and monitors and buttons and options than the control board in Jay-Z's recording studio. You still see a preponderance of women and the elderly playing the slots. (Those buses with the names of retirement homes in casino parking lots aren't delivering hold 'em players to the tables.) But you also see younger couples, drawn to the lure of the progressive slots and to high-tech computerized machines featuring their favorite TV shows and movies.

I have never understood the appeal of the slots. You sit on your stool, you pull the lever or you press the button, you watch the wheels go round and round—and either you win or the machine goes silent.

And then you do it again.

And again.

And again.

Is there anything more mind numbing and soul crushing than the slots? You see these slots players in their logo sweatshirts and their comfortable pants and gym shoes, camped out in front of their favorite machines as they suck on their cigarettes and rattle the ice in their drinks, their eyes glazing as they stare straight ahead. It's as if they're hypnotized. Sometimes they don't move for hours. Hardcore slots players are extremely territorial creatures who love to find a quiet, dark corner of a casino to set up shop. They will zealously guard their turf, and they'll hit you with an icy glare if you even sit next to them. Don't you know they're playing *both* of those machines, and they've invested hours of time and hundreds of dollars in their quest to hit the jackpot, which is "due" any time now!

And yet I know some bright, inquisitive, interesting people who absolutely love the slots. A friend of mine who works in an extremely

stressful field puts it this way: "I can sit at the Wheel of Fortune machine and just zone out. I usually win just enough to keep playing for an hour, maybe two, and then I take a break and grab a bite and come back for another couple of hours. I've never won or lost all that much money. If I hit a terrible losing streak, I walk away. If I win $300, I stop. If I'm playing blackjack, I have to stay in the game and make a decision every 30 seconds. It's not a particularly taxing decision, but it's enough to keep me from totally relaxing. Not so with the slots. With the slots, I can just get lost in the game without having to do much of anything."

A couple of years ago, I was walking through the hallway at the Caesars Palace in Elizabeth, Indiana, shortly after arriving on the property on a Friday morning. I happened upon a long row of wheelchairs—doublewide wheelchairs. An employee explained that many of their customers were simply too large to fit into normal-sized chairs—and too sedentary to make the long trek from the hotel to the casino. All day long, you'd see casino employees literally wheeling gamblers to their favorite slot machines. Folks, that's not too far from the dark future of the movie *Wall-E*, with all those humans who were too big and slovenly to get around on their own.

Monkeys could be trained to play the slots. Dogs, too. I'm reasonably certain even a few species of crustaceans could pull it off. I know there are slots tournaments, and I know there are dedicated slots players who will tell you there's an art to picking the right machine, real skill involved in knowing how much to bet and how many lines to play, and actual science to playing those "progressive" slots—and I still say all you're doing is methodically pushing a button as if you're in an early episode of *Lost*.

To me the slots are a whim, a nod to the madness and folly of gambling. Over the years when I've been in Vegas with a group of roustabouts, there will inevitably come a time when I'll announce my traditional visit to the high-limit slots area. (This moment usually comes after a considerable number of powerful beverages.) We'll traipse over to a $25 or a $100 machine, I'll insert three or four hondos—and in less time than it has taken you to read this paragraph, the money will disappear, as if I've just flushed it down the drain. Every once in a great while, I'll win $500 or so, at which point I'll print out my winning voucher and we'll all run away from the slots area as if a fire has broken out. And then I'll buy a few more rounds of drinks for everyone.

If there's someone new in our group, he or she will marvel at the madness of sticking a $100 bill into a machine that gobbles it up like a shark swallowing chum. It's such an instantaneous, obscenely dull waste of $100—money that could be spent on groceries or bills or a charitable donation or life in general. Even when you win, there's none of the jolt you get when your team covers the spread or you hit a hard 10 at the craps table or you go all-in with the best hand at a poker tournament. There's a lot of clanging and whirring from the machine, but you know the machine doesn't mean it—and you know it was pure, 100 percent luck that gave you this jackpot. Didn't have a damn thing to do with you.

The slots also have murderous odds.

If you can count cards at blackjack or you have the stamina and the knowledge to play perfect video poker over an extended period of time, you might be able to eke out a very tiny edge over the house. I'm talking about maybe 1 percent.

In all other casino games, the house has a decided edge, ranging from 1 or 2 percent if you play smart craps to 25 to 29 percent if you're insane enough to play keno. (Don't play keno. And by the way: don't play keno. Just come over to my house and hand me your money, and I'll hold onto it until your urge to play keno subsides.)

With the slots, the higher the denomination you play, the better your odds. If you're playing a $100 slot machine, the house has an edge of about 4 percent. If you're playing a nickel slot machine, their advantage shoots up to about 15 percent.

This is the thing that kills me about the slots: the casinos tell you they're going to take your money. They advertise it!

You see those billboards claiming a 97 percent return on the slots, as if that's a good thing. Well, it's better than 85 percent or 92 percent—but it's still an open admission that over the long run, you simply cannot win.

The laws vary from state to state, but there's always a minimum percentage the casinos must pay out on the slots. In general, you'll get from 85 percent to 90 percent return on your money. But just because a casino claims a 97 percent return doesn't mean all machines are equal. That's the maximum you'll get if you play the maximum amount of money on the high-stakes machines.

But even then, you're looking at a return of 97 cents on every dollar you wager. Imagine if you walked into a bank and they were advertising the same deal: "Deposit $100 with us and you'll average a $97 return on your investment! You'll lose only three dollars!" Um, what?

Let's say you're playing a $1 slot machine with a 90 percent return. In the course of an average hour, you're going to lose about $48. Even if you're playing a quarter slot machine with that return, you're looking at a loss of $12 per hour.

The key for the casinos is to give you just enough incentive to keep playing. On the Wheel of Fortune game, you "come close" to hitting the big numbers on the wheel so many times that you feel the machine is "due," even though the machine is a computer with no memory and has been calibrated to come oh-so-close to hitting the big numbers time and again. At the $5 machines, you win just enough to stick around. If you lost $100 in the first five minutes every time you played, you'd give up the slots. But if you're up a few hundred, then down a bit, then up again, then near even, and it takes an hour or two to lose that $100, you somehow feel as if you got your money's worth. You feel as if you just might beat that machine next time. "I was almost there!" you'll say. Uh-huh.

For these reasons and more, I've never entered a casino with the specific purpose of playing the slots. If slot machines were the only option available in the world of gambling, I'd be writing a book about coffee or something right now. But for the purposes of this adventure, today is Slots Day. *Woohooooooo!*

It's a suitably rainy weekday afternoon as I make the drive north to Elgin—home of that man who was sentenced to four years in prison for operating Super Bowl pools—and the Grand Victoria Casino, a perfectly nice and well-run establishment that nevertheless gives off a vibe of malaise as I enter.

I'm greeted by a sign that proclaims:

YOUR BILLS, ON US.
Play Grand Victoria and win your share of $300,000 to pay your bills with!

Each drawing day, 15 players will win guaranteed cash prizes and a chance at the $36,000 grand prize!

To play, join Club Victoria. It's free and you'll receive five free entries just for signing up. Drawings are . . . throughout March at 2 p.m., 6 p.m. and 8 p.m.

In these harsh economic times, I'm surprised a casino would even want to mention the word *bills* in a promotion. Let's face it, more than a few gamers in any casino are risking money that should be going toward the rent and the utilities and the groceries and clothes for the kids. They're trying to double or triple their paychecks, in the hopes of making a dent in that MasterCard bill or getting the roof fixed. On a recent Friday night at a casino in northwest Indiana, I was stunned at the sheer numbers of gamblers. The place was bursting with action, as if they were making a movie and an overzealous casting director had gone overboard with the number of extras. It was the only time in my life I'd ever seen lines six deep at the ATMs in a casino. When I mentioned this to a friend of mine who runs a business in the area, he offered an explanation: "It was payday. A lot of those people had just cashed their checks. By Saturday morning, a lot of them will be kicking themselves and trying to figure out how they're going to make it to the next payday." (By the way, try not to use ATMs in casinos. For one thing, it means you've lost the money you brought with you and you're probably not going to win it back. Also, most casino ATMs charge about double the fee you'd pay at a regular ATM. Some will charge as much as 3.5 percent of the money you're taking out. Others will hit you with flat fee of $25 or more.)

This afternoon at the Grand Victoria, the bar and the restaurants are just about empty, but the casino is doing brisk business. There's steady action at the craps and blackjack tables, and a few cash games underway in the small poker area downstairs.

I find an open seat at the $5 slots and insert three $100 bills. A little sign on my machine tells me the Grand Victoria has been "Voted Best Reel Slots." OK. I guess I missed that particular election.

Even though the lever will set the reels in motion, nobody pulls the lever any more. You press the button. Pulling the lever identifies you as an utter novice. It takes more time to pull the lever. It takes more effort to pull the lever. Think about that: the act of reaching up and pulling a lever was deemed too much of a physical challenge and too much of a time-waster for the average slots player, so they made it easier for us by giving buttons to push. Why raise your arm when all you have to do is move a finger?

Every time I push the button, it's a $5 bet. Within the first 20 minutes, I'm down $150. A 50ish woman in a Bears jersey sidles up and stands over me, watching me in action. Whatever I'm doing, she's not impressed. She walks away.

Between spins, I observe the scene around me. Nobody smiles when playing the slots. There's very little conversation. There's none of that charged-up energy you experience at craps or even blackjack or roulette, when it's "us" against the house, and for the most part everyone is rooting for everyone else. Like video poker, this is a solitary experience designed to separate you from any social interaction—which may be why so many people prefer the slots. You don't have to think. You don't have to socialize. You don't have to do anything but push a button and zone out.

I move from the $5 slots to the $1 machines to the so-called penny slots, and we'll get into that racket in a moment. The machines carry promises—warnings? rules?—that go like this: "Any combination of 4 Double 7 or Double or Double Bar pays 16x winning combination, except when 5 symbols with Double are sharing one payline."

Right. Of course. Like I didn't know that.

After the first hour of play, I'm somehow up $154. I'm at a $5 machine and I go to the "Maximum Credits" option, which means I'm now risking $15 a spin. In less than 10 minutes, I lose $200.

I circle around a bit and settle on a 25¢ slot machine with a Golden Pyramids theme. Some slot machines feature video clips and sophisticated artwork; others, like this one, feature basic animation and crude illustrations straight out of a children's book.

When I win 60 credits ($15), the machine says, "You Little Devil!" When I win 75 credits, it issues a challenge: "I'd Like to See That Again!"

With each spin, little icons whiz by: the Taj Mahal, an elephant, a monkey. I have no idea what all this means. I'm pretty sure it's a good thing when the cartoon princess shows up. What I do know is that I'm on a bit of a hot streak. I hit a 5x winner, than an 80x winner. I'm up about $700. A man with thick glasses and a shocking amount of hair sprouting from his ears comes over to watch me play. I try to engage him in conversation. He seems shocked I'd talk to him and he scurries away.

I print out my voucher and move on. (The days of silver dollars or gold coins cascading onto a tray beneath the slots are long gone. You don't insert coins into the modern slot machine; you insert bills or vouchers. When you hit a jackpot, the machine will make that famil-

iar "payout" sound, as if coins are dropping, but it's the equivalent of an iPhone with an application that makes it sound like an old-fashioned phone when it rings. It's a special effect. When you hit the "Cash Out" button on a slot machine, it just prints out a voucher.)

Time to try my luck at the 2¢ slots. It seems incongruous that so many casinos have penny slots and 2¢ slots in the 21st century—but these types of machines are hugely popular nowadays, probably more so than ever before. There's a whole penny-slot renaissance. That's because hardly anybody is playing just a penny a spin at the penny slots. You can play 3, 5, 10, 20, even a hundred or more credits with every spin. Put a $100 bill in a penny slot machine and you'll get 10,000 credits—but you can risk hundreds of credits every spin, and that $100 will eventually disappear, credit by credit by credit. Players who wouldn't think of trying the $5 slots ("That's way too rich for my blood!") will sit at a 2¢ slot machine, believing it's well within their means—and it would be, if they risked just two pennies with each spin. They'd probably get carpal tunnel syndrome before they'd lose a hundred bucks. But they start playing 10 credits per spin—hey, that's still just 20 cents—and then 20 or 30 or 40 credits per spin, because they're not going to win the big jackpot if they won't play multiple lines. Next thing they know, they *are* risking $5 per spin. The machine is just phrasing it differently.

I'm playing the S&H Green Stamps machine. Talk about a nostalgia trip! Although the slots are computerized, state-of-the-art machines, the artwork is straight out of the 1950s and 1960s—icons depicting old-fashioned toasters and cameras, a guy who looks like the Organization Man, toy cars.

For $100, I get 5,000 credits. At one point I win 1,460 credits on one spin and the machine goes crazy, drawing the momentary attention of some of my fellow 2¢ slot players. Jackpot! *Ding-ding-ding-ding-ding!* A tiny display in the lower left corner delivers the final total: I just won, um, $73. Oh. Seemed like a lot more when it was 1,460 credits.

I start playing the maximum amount on multiple lines, turning this 2¢ slot machine into a dollar slot machine—and I lose $100 in exactly six minutes. Time to move again. I head downstairs and grab a drink at the bar, where a waitress is lamenting the tip situation as a sympathetic bartender listens. You've got to figure someone working the weekday mid-afternoon shift at this casino isn't coming home with fistfuls of cash and probably isn't fulfilling her childhood dreams, God love her. Yet if she quit, there would probably be a dozen applicants hoping against hope to get that job.

Down about $300 total, I sit down at a machine called Dean Martin's Wild Party. It's a 5¢ slot, licensed by the Dean Martin Family Trust, with artwork of dice, cards, a 1950s-era cocktail waitress—and a giant photo of Dean's head placed atop a little cartoon body.

Dean's recorded voice emanates from the jukebox:

How lucky can one guy be?
I kissed her and she kissed me
Like the fella once said
Ain't that a kick in the head?

You think of Dean Martin singing with the Rat Pack in Vegas in the early 1960s. All those famous photos of Dean and Sammy and Frank and Joey Bishop and Peter Lawford onstage at the Sands, wearing tuxedos, cigarettes and cocktails in hands, exuding the ultimate in hipster cool. Now they're all gone, and the likeness and voice of Dean Martin are on a 5¢ slot machine on the bottom floor of a riverboat casino in Elgin, Illinois. There's something beyond melancholy about that.

When I hit a winner, Dean sings, "Don't stop, don't stop, go, go, go, go." When I'm a loser, Dean has nothing to say and nothing to sing.

So long, Dean.

After three-plus hours of play at nearly a dozen different slot machines, I'm down maybe a hundred bucks. I consider this a victory, as I expected to lose the full grand for the day.

On the way out of the casino, I spot the high-limit area.

Gotta do it.

I insert a $100 bill into a $25 slot machine, electing to play one credit at a time.

The first two spins yield nothing but silence. I'm standing at the machine with jacket on, ready to play two more spins and head for the parking lot.

I hit the button again, the icons start spinning—and when they click to a stop, the lights start flashing and the music starts playing, and the credits start climbing . . .

I've just won $3,000. Well, that's just great. I've gone and killed my whole chapter on how the slots are the worst play in the casino.

An attendant shuffles over, reads the screen, and says, "Nice!" He takes my identification, says he'll have to get a manager, and invites me to take a seat, as this will take a few minutes.

When you win big, it always takes a few minutes if not longer to get paid. When you lose, that doesn't take any time at all.

A waitress comes over and hands me a Heineken. I sip my beer and chuckle at the folly of the slots.

After a few minutes, an Executive Host comes over and congratulates me and hands me a tax form. The first attendant who came over is back as well, grinning broadly at me as if we've just pulled off some kind of a heist. The Executive Host explains there must be two witnesses present for the actual payout.

OK. Then we just stand there for a moment, until I realize I'm supposed to put my hand out, like I'm receiving communion at church. The Executive Host counts out $3,000 in $100 bills and asks why I didn't tell them I was coming in today. (I'm not exactly Ashton Kutcher, but because I've been on TV, I do get recognized once or twice a day. For most of my gambling adventures, I've taken to wearing a baseball cap and sporting an unshaven look, so I can have the experience without the distraction of talking about movies or getting any kind of special treatment. Occasionally, though, someone will stop and ask me how the book is coming or ask me to take a picture with them.) Had they known I was coming, well, then they would have known I was coming.

A **$3,000** winner at the slot machines.

After the little ceremony ends, I realize I still have $50 in credit with the machine. As if to remind myself the slots are a bad bet, I play two credits on one spin and watch the $50 disappear in a split second.

Told you the slots are a terrible play.

Day 7

**Bankroll:
+$2,870**

"In my experience, there is no such thing as luck."
—Obi-Wan Kenobi

Everywhere you look, somebody's offering you the opportunity to take a chance and win big. Even Hannah Montana.

On a windy spring day, I'm filling the gas tank at a BP station in northern Indiana, reading the green-and-yellow sign above the pumps:

YOU COULD WIN GAS FOR A YEAR AND MORE
Pump 5 gallons or more of gasoline, bring your receipt to the cashier and receive a little better game™ card. Scratch to reveal if you're an instant winner! Additional prizes include trips to a Disney movie premiere or a trip to the Walt Disney Studios, Miley Cyrus autographed memorabilia, Hannah Montana™ DVDs and CDs and BP Gift Cards!

BP celebrates the magic of Disney movies with over 100 exciting prizes from "Hannah Montana: The Movie."

But if I'm buying gas in order to enter a contest, doesn't that make it a gambling pool? In order for this to be a sweepstakes, don't we need the old "No purchase necessary" clause?

Sure enough, there's a way to play the game without purchasing gas. All you have to do is "send a hand-printed, self-addressed, postage-stamped #10 envelope with sufficient postage" to a post office box in Elmhurst, Illinois, and they'll send you one game card, while supplies last. That's the same old-school method they used for sweepstakes back in the 1960s and 1970s. I wonder how many people are actually filling out self-addressed stamped envelopes these days. The over/under on that has to be about 6.

The biggest prize in this sweepstakes is a trip to a movie premiere—not necessarily the *Hannah Montana* movie, mind you, but a flick of the Sponsor's choosing. (It brings to mind the old joke: First prize is two tickets to the next *Fast and Furious* movie. Second prize is four tickets.)

Odds of winning the movie premiere package: 1 in 5.33 million.

As for "gas for a year," BP has determined that would cost exactly $2,080, and they'll pay it out in the form of BP gift cards. That's based on "16 gallons purchased per week at $2.50 per gallon over the duration of one year." Obviously a truck driver or even someone who commutes 50 miles roundtrip per day to work would have a different definition of "gas for a year."

I fill my tank and head inside to the little store—the same kind of store you see at most interstate gas stations these days. There's a staggering array of bottled and canned cold drinks on refrigerated shelves (are we all that thirsty all the time?); racks of candy and cookies and potato chips and beef jerky and other junk foods; magazines and maps; coffee in a variety of flavors; key chains and snow globes and other knick-knacks; and a rack of T-shirts, sweatshirts, and hats. Who buys clothes at the gas station—Thelma and Louise?

Of course, the other thing you can buy at the gas station is a lottery ticket.

I started out the morning with a purchase of about $200 worth of lottery tickets at a 7-Eleven in downtown Chicago, and now I'm making my way across Indiana and into Michigan, with several stops along the way to buy different types of lottery tickets.

Yes, today is lottery day. As is the case with the slots, I'm entering territory that's largely foreign to me. I've purchased maybe $200 worth of lottery tickets in my entire life, usually when a Powerball prize has reached such an insanely high level that everyone's talking about it and you just want in on the dream.

Because that's what you're doing when you buy a lottery ticket—you're purchasing the rights to a fantasy for a day or a week. You've got a tangible excuse to let your mind run wild with thoughts of quitting your job, paying off every bill, helping out your family, and buying a house in the tropics, where you'll spend the rest of your days living like a character in a Corona commercial.

That's as far as it goes for 99.9 percent of us—the dream. Cuz you ain't gonna win. Ever. You know that, right?

It has often been said the odds of winning a major lottery prize are about the same as one getting struck by lightning, but in fact your chances of getting zapped are greater than your chances of winning Powerball.

The exact odds of winning a mega-zega-trega-million-dollar lottery prize vary, but usually your chances are about 1 in 75 million. Good luck with that.

Odds of getting struck by lightning: 1 in 12 million. So you're about six times more likely to get struck by lightning. You also have a "better" chance of being poisoned, dying in a plane crash, getting electrocuted, or freezing to death, and why are we using such horrible analogies to illustrate the point?

All right, let's go the other way. Each year, *Playboy* has 12 Playmates of the Month. Some of them wind up living with Hugh Hefner and pretending he's not 154 years old, others are drawn into Pauly

Shore's mysteriously powerful web of sexual intrigue—but eventually nearly all of them get married. If we take the pool of eligible adult males in the United States, you have maybe a 1 in 3 million shot of marrying a *Playboy* Playmate, if that's the sort of thing you'd like to fantasize about.

Heck, based on Angelina Jolie's romantic track record to date, including long-term relationships and marriages, you have a better chance of becoming romantically involved with Angelina Jolie than you do of winning the Powerball. You probably even have a better chance of marrying Angelina Jolie on the day you're getting sworn in as a United States senator.

Yet millions of Americans play the lottery every day. Walk into any gas station or convenience store in the country, and there's a good chance someone will be standing there, robotically reciting numbers from a piece of paper to a clerk working the lottery computer. Or they're handing over their tickets from the day before to see how much they've won.

And what do they do if the clerk informs them they've come out $20 or $30 ahead? They use their winnings to buy more lottery tickets.

By the time I reach Benton Harbor, Michigan, the large envelope in the back seat is bulging with "live" tickets promising untold riches. And in addition to the $800 or so worth of lottery tickets I've purchased in Illinois, Indiana, and Michigan, friends in Texas, New York, and California have bought tickets for me today, just to spread the losses—I mean, the chances—around.

I've got dozens and dozens of cardboard instant play tickets—those scratch-off cards that leave tiny pieces of gun-metal-gray shavings all over the place as you feverishly rub a nickel over the darkened areas to see if you're a winner. Most of these cards have artwork that's something out of a hipster animated cartoon: color schemes dominated by bright greens and reds and blues and purples and big fat lettering. The names are reminiscent of the English wording you see on products in foreign countries, as if someone who's not in complete command of the language has dreamed them up:

- Lucky Bet
- $500 Fury
- Golden 7s
- Money Mania Millions
- Million Dollar Madness
- All the Marbles
- Platinum 8s
- Winner's Wonderland
- 8 Ball Bingo
- Million Dollar Megaplay

The state of Michigan has a Three Stooges game. It plays like most other scratch-off games, only there's a photo of Larry, Moe, and Curly in wrestling attire on the card. Apparently that ancient celebrity tie-in will attract a certain segment of lottery players.

There would appear to be an endless array of scratch-off games, but they're all pretty much the same. You're trying to match a number, or beat a number, or duplicate a certain symbol three times in a row, in order to win a designated prize. In Casino Action, you're rubbing off numbers in a blackjack game and trying to beat the dealer, who never busts and rarely has a hand lower than 19. If you get a 20 or a 21, it's almost certain your prize is $1 or $2. If you get a 13, a.k.a. a loser hand—that's when the attendant prize you *didn't* win would have been $1,000 or more.

In New Buffalo, Michigan, I pull into a parking lot of an establishment that appears to have gone out of business just recently. The lot is empty; there's no sign of life inside. A sign stretching high into the sky features the Ace of hearts and the Jack of spades, along with the name of the joint:

CASINO PIZZERIA
WE DELIVER

Wait a minute. A place called Casino Pizzeria couldn't make it? You're serving up America's favorite food as well as America's favorite pastime, and you're out of business? If a pizzeria/casino can't survive, the economy really is in the toilet.

Well. Turns out Casino Pizzeria was so named because it was just around the corner from the sprawling Four Winds Casino. It was just a pizzeria. They didn't have slots in there or anything. (Although there's an idea for somebody.)

I turn up the satellite radio and roll down the windows, get out of the car, envelope in hand, and take a seat on my trunk. This seems like a good spot to start scratching through the thick, three-state stack of lottery tickets. Come on, Curly, Moe, and Larry! Show me a winner.

The government runs lotteries with more efficiency and with more of a self-made advantage—and on a much grander scale—than any mobster ever displayed while running a numbers game.

Let's say you buy a lottery ticket and you play the birthdays of your wife and your children, plus your Little League number. On the morning after the drawing, the TV news anchor says, "There was only one winner in last night's lottery, and the winning ticket was bought in suburban Riverdale. . . ."

Wait a minute. *You* bought your ticket in suburban Riverdale.

You check your numbers against the winning ticket. Match, match, match, match . . .

Holy cow! You're a winner! You've just won $10 million.

Well. Sort of.

First you have to decide if you want a lump-sum payment or an annuity, paid out over 20 or 25 years. If you go for the annuity and it's a 20-year payment, you'd get $500,000 a year for 20 years—before taxes.

If you go for the lump sum, you don't get $10 million—you get $5 million, even though the grand prize in our mythical lottery was advertised everywhere as $10 million. That's because the fine print says the grand prize is based on the annuity. (Most big jackpot winners opt for the lump sum. They figure they'll get a better return on their own investments instead of relying on a steady annuity. Of course, the bigger the initial prize, the more you're going to be hearing from fleece artists and friends you never knew you had, offering to help you invest all that money.)

After state and federal taxes are taken off the top, your take-home prize would be a little more than $2.5 million. That's a sweet payday—but it's not $10 million, is it?

Not that you're going to win anyway.

There is nothing Zen about scratching off ticket after ticket after ticket. There sure as shit isn't any skill involved. You just fall into a funk where you expect to lose—and when you win, you know it's going to be for a lesser denomination. Out of hundreds of tickets purchased in more than a half-dozen states, the biggest single winner I had was $30—and that was on a $10 ticket.

I've also got hundreds of tickets for Mega Millions, Little Lotto, Powerball, and other big-jackpot games. You don't have to check your numbers against the winning numbers online or in the newspaper—you just bring your tix to any store where they sell lottery tickets and they'll scan 'em for you.

I win $93 in one game, $85 on another.

All told, I purchased about $1,400 in lottery tickets and experienced a net loss of nearly $1,100. I'm surprised I did that well.

Driving back to Chicago, I make a last-minute decision to stop at a casino in northwest Indiana to play some good old-fashioned blackjack.

Just some of the lottery tickets I bought. There's not a golden ticket in the bunch.

The ATM dispenses 10 crisp $100 bills. Every other ATM in the world maxes out at $20 denominations. In a casino ATM, you get hundreds.

It's a weekday evening, and the place is humming with action. I find a seat at a blackjack table with only one smoker (unlike Illinois, Indiana has yet to pass a comprehensive antismoking bill, so you can still fire up in bars and restaurants and casinos), exchange my $1,000 in cash for $500 in green $25 chips and $500 in black $100 chips, place two greens on the circle in front of me, and here we go.

Two hours later, I'm up about $3,000. I've had swings where I've been down as much as $800 and up as much as $5,000, but I've never had to dip into my pocket for more cash. It's one of those sessions where you win three, lose one, win four, lose two, win six. When I double down, I get the 10 I'm supposed to get. When I stand on 14 when the dealer shows a 3, he busts, like he's supposed to do. Every once in a while, I get a blackjack with its lovely 3-2 payout. Whenever that happens, I put a green chip in front of the three black chips I'm playing—that's a bet for the dealer. If I win, the dealer—or more accurately, all the dealers who are working this particular shift, as they normally pool their tips—gets a $50 tip. If I lose, the dealer taps the chip against the felt, thanks me for the bet, and drops it into the house tray.

I make a vow to stop playing if I lose three hands in a row. That doesn't happen for another half hour or so. When it does, when my 20 gets beaten by a 10-6-5 for a 21, I stand up and ask to be "colored up," that satisfying ritual where they take your greens and your blacks and give you pink $500 chips and yellow $1,000 chips. It's off to the cashier, who will turn those clay chips into a nice stack of $100 bills.

The lottery? You might as well take a match to your money. Blackjack is for the real players. And for this one night at least, I feel like a real player. A hot session like that makes you forget about every losing streak, every bad beat, every time you've actually blamed the dealer for giving you terrible cards, as if he or she has any control over it. I'm in northwest Indiana on a chilly spring night, but as I walk through the casino, I feel like I'm Bond in Monte Carlo. I feel as if there's no easier way to make money than by placing $100 chips in a circle, glancing at my cards, and telling the dealer, "Hit me."

The Best Gambling Movies of All Time

From *Guys and Dolls* to *21*, from *The Cincinnati Kid* to *Rounders*, Hollywood has given us dozens of movies about gamblers and the world of gambling. Most of the best gambling movies are journeys to the dark side—character studies of wounded outcasts who are hooked on cards, dice, or sports betting. But I did find room on my list for a couple of lighthearted romps as well.

1. *The Gambler* (1974): James Toback's screenplay perfectly captures the mind-set of the self-destructive gambler. James Caan deserved an Oscar nomination for his intense performance as a college professor who is addicted to the thrill of the bet. The most devastating ending ever in a gambling film.

2. *Rounders* (1998): You'd be hard-pressed to find a poker pro that *doesn't* list this film as the best and most accurate depiction of the poker world. Features a first-rate script filled with quotable lines, great performances from Matt Damon and Edward Norton, and a thrilling (albeit over-

the-top) heads-up Texas hold 'em confrontation between Damon and John Malkovich.

3. *California Split* (1974): This underrated classic from Robert Altman is a bittersweet dissection of a friendship based on one common bond: mutual love of gambling. Elliott Gould and George Segal are in top form as the gambling buddies.

4. *The Hustler* (1961) and *The Color of Money* (1986): Paul Newman is riveting, whether he's the young Fast Eddie playing Minnesota Fats for $3,000 a game in the original, or the much older Eddie schooling Tom Cruise and feeling the hustle from Forest Whitaker in the sequel.

5. *Casino* (1995): Martin Scorsese's period-piece classic provides a fascinating behind-the-scenes look at the coolly efficient and sometimes chillingly ruthless methods of the old-school casino bosses.

6. *The Cooler* (2003): A dark fable from Wayne Kramer with a brilliant performance by William H. Macy as a lifelong loser employed by the casino to use his anti–Midas touch on hot gamblers. By merely brushing against someone who's on a winning streak, Macy can cool him down. Alec Baldwin shines as a cutthroat casino boss resisting the overtures of the young suits who want to take over his joint.

7. *Hard Eight* (1996): Philip Baker Hall is a world-weary gambler in Reno who takes young John C. Reilly under his wing. There are a couple of great twists and turns in this gambling noir film, which also features a young Gwyneth Paltrow and a menacing Samuel L. Jackson.

8. *Owning Mahowny* (2003): The best depiction of the wagering addict since *The Gambler*, with Philip Seymour Hoffman expertly conveying the desperation of a man whose gambling has taken over his life, setting off a chain of events from which there is no turning back.

9. *Let It Ride* (1989): Slapstick farce with a wildly entertaining performance by Richard Dreyfuss as a horse player who finally has that one day every gambler dreams of, when everything he touches turns to gold.

10. *The Sting* (1973): A cheeky romp with a gambling-related con-job-within-a-con-job. Paul Newman and Robert Redford are charming rogues, and Robert Shaw is the snarling villain. The last act features a fascinating extended set-up—and a payoff that stunned and delighted audiences in 1973.

Honorable mention: *The Cincinnati Kid;** Bob the Gambler; The Only Game in Town; High Roller: The Stu Ungar Story; Kaleidoscope; Croupier; The Good Thief; Lock, Stock and Two Smoking Barrels; House of Games.*

---

* As much as I love *The Cincinnati Kid*, it's not on the top 10 list because it's essentially the same movie as *The Hustler*, with five-card stud replacing pool. Also, the famous final hand is cartoonishly ludicrous. The odds of one player getting a straight flush and one player getting a full house in a heads-up game of five-card stud are 45 million to 1.

Day 8

Bankroll:
+$4,980

"Money won is twice as sweet as money earned."
—*The Color of Money*

When I got back to Chicago last night, I was too wired from the blackjack run to turn in, so I texted around until I found a couple of friends who were hanging at the Kerryman, less than two blocks from my house.

This is the blessing, and also the curse, of living in the heart of one of the city's busiest areas: there's never a shortage of places to go and people to meet. The Kerryman, a two-story Irish pub and restaurant with outdoor seating when the weather permits, is just one of about two dozen restaurants and bars within a few blocks' walk from my place. (It was a favorite haunt of Johnny Depp's when he was in town filming *Public Enemies*.) My options include genuine Irish bars like Celtic Crossings, where there are no TVs and there's often a trio there playing live music; another Irish pub/restaurant called Garret Ripley's; and the Clark Street Ale House, which allows dogs to roam freely in the bar and is known for the refreshingly blunt message on the neon

sign out front: STOP AND DRINK. A recent addition to the neighborhood: the nightclub Angels & Kings, owned in part by Pete Wentz.

So I met up with my friends at the Kerryman, and they were bonding with two young women from Philadelphia who were in town for a sales convention. The women wanted to see what Angels & Kings was like, so we stopped for there for a nightcap, and I left when everyone started doing shots of tequila, because I had a very early wake-up call to appear on *The Howard Stern Show.*

When I drew the loose outline for this 30-day adventure, one of the elements I wanted to include was a bet with Artie Lange, the grizzled, corpulent, multiply addicted, and hilarious comic who has been a regular on the Stern show for nearly a decade now. In the jaw-droppingly dark reality show that is Artie's life—which almost became an actual reality show, until Artie thought better of it and turned down the deal—he often tells stories on the air about his gambling adventures, whether he's winning a small fortune at blackjack, trying to figure out how to handle the situation with a bookie who won't pay him, or lamenting a losing weekend of football bets. A few days earlier, I had talked to Stern's producer, Gary Dell'Abate (forever known as "Baba Booey"), explained the book to him, and pitched the idea of making an on-air bet with Artie.

"I love it," said Gary. "Let's set something up for this week."

While I was on the road buying lottery tickets, I did a pre-interview with segment producer Will Murray and told him about some of my experiences to date, including the $3,000 win on the slots. We were all set for this morning's interview, to take place at 6:30 A.M. my time, which means I had to get up at about 6 A.M., about four hours after I left Angels & Kings.

Orange juice. Tylenol. Water. Time for a mad dash to Starbucks? No. Get stuck behind one early riser who's picking up lattes for the whole office and you won't have enough time to make it back.

For the last few years, Stern's show has been on satellite radio, which means you have to pay a subscription fee to hear him. Although Howard's audience isn't as large as it was when he was on terrestrial radio and he was syndicated to most major markets, millions of hardcore fans still tune in every day. I've been a guest on the Stern show maybe a half dozen times, and I was judge for the first (and to date the only) Howard Stern Festival in New York City a few years back, and every time I make an appearance, I hear from legions of listeners for weeks afterward. If Howard likes you—and he's always been great to me—they like you. If Howard turns on you, God help you. I know of celebrities who have humbly called in to Stern's show to mend fences because they just couldn't take the constant harassment from Stern's army of loyal fans.

Howard was still on K-Rock when I first appeared on the show, with Roger Ebert. Roger was sure Howard was going to goof on me. "Usually he's on me about my weight," said Roger, "but you're the new guy and he'll be all over you."

Instead, Howard introduced me and announced, "I approve of your choice for the new cohost, Roger." Sweet.

Like any other guest on Stern's show, I've had those moments where you feel as if you're levitating above yourself, looking down on the poor schmuck who's being grilled by Howard Stern. There was the time Stern went through a list of names, asking me if I'd slept with any of these women. (In one case, the answer was yes. I lied through my teeth and said no, I don't even know her.) And there was an unfortunate series of circumstances on Howard's show that led to the infamous Page Six of the *New York Post* running a couple of items about me that didn't necessarily please my bosses at Disney, even though the behavior ascribed to me wasn't necessarily true and wouldn't have been illegal anyway, and I'll just leave it at that.

But Stern and his team have also said a lot of kind things about me, and they promote the hell out of your book, your TV show, your Web site. I don't necessarily want to be in the studio when one of Howard's comedic henchmen is getting his genital area waxed or some dimwit porn star is riding an automated sex machine, but if you stay true to yourself and you remember everything you say will be used against you (or to your benefit) for Pop Culture Eternity, there's no better guesting experience.

It happens once in every 650,000 hands—a royal flush in Texas hold 'em. I got this one in a home game.

Howard starts the phone interview by talking about how much he admires Roger Ebert and how strong Roger has been through his health problems. We talk a little bit about why I left the movie show and what I'm doing now, which leads to a discussion of the book. Howard tells his audience that if the book was supposed to be a cautionary tale, it's not working, because I'm winning. I tell the story about my jackpot win at the Grand Victoria, but I also caution that it's still early and there's plenty of time for me to hit a losing streak. I'm flush off my blackjack triumph and I don't necessarily believe that, but no point in sounding too cocky.

Howard says, "Is it true you got a royal flush in a poker game?"

Indeed it is. It happened just the other night during one of my regular home poker games. (About 20 players, everyone puts in $300, top three or four get paid.) I was dealt J-10 of spades. Player to my right had pocket Kings. He raised; I called.

The flop was A-K-2. All spades. That gave him a set of Kings but gave me the flush—and the turn was the Queen of spades, giving me the royal. I didn't win a ton of money on the pot, but as far as I can remember, it was the first time I ever got a royal flush in a live game. (I've gotten a couple online.) You have a 0.000154 percent chance of getting a royal flush on any given hand of hold 'em.

(I also got a straight flush in video poker while in Vegas on day 4. It was one of those deals where I went to the bar during a break in the real poker tournament, ordered a Bloody Mary, and put a few bucks into one of the video poker machines conveniently embedded in the surface of the bar. I drew to a straight flush and it hit, good for $250. Although I'm not recounting every single wager in this book, I am keeping track of all bets large and small, including home poker games and incidental wagers like the video poker game. It all counts toward the final bankroll total.)

Video poker isn't my game, but I'll take a straight flush any time.

I make my proposition to Artie. He can have his pick of any of the NCAA games tonight, $1,000 straight up. For real money. Loser has to send the winner a check.

It takes Artie about a 10th of a second to say he's up for it—and he knows which team he's going to take. Artie says he loves Memphis State giving 4½ to Missouri.

OK, but shit. I had Memphis State underlined as one of the picks I wanted to make tonight. But that's the bet, so I say, "You're on. Go Tigers!" which is a little confusing given that both teams are nicknamed the Tigers, but there you have it. I've got Mizzou plus the 4½ for a grand. And because I've got that gambler's mentality that says if you're going to go big with a bet you might as well go bigger, lest you regret not putting more on it when you *do* win, I call Sid the Bookie and put another dime on Missouri, giving me a total of $2,000 on the game.

A game I do not watch.

About an hour before the Missouri-Memphis game tips off, I'm at the bar of a downtown Chicago hotel, nursing a Stella Artois and waiting for my appointment to show up. We've met briefly in person a few times and those encounters were a few years ago—but there's no mistaking her as she enters the room, turning heads and gracefully ignoring the stares with the poise of someone who has been drawing hard looks for most of her life.

I could tell you this woman is extremely bright and funny and interesting because that's all true, but that's not what people see when

they first meet her. They see one of the most attractive human beings on the planet. There's pretty and there's gorgeous, and then there are women who look like this.

This is not a date. We are getting together because she's helping to organize a private cash poker game, to be held in a city I will not name in a hotel I will not name, involving some players you'd know if I mentioned their names. Sorry to be so cryptic, but we're talking about a game in which the initial buy-in is in five figures, and there's no limit to the amount of cash you can bring.

It's beyond my level. For one thing, I could lose the entire stake for this book in a couple of minutes. Besides, if you're playing with guys who can afford to drop a few hundred thousand dollars in a night without blinking, and they're comfortable with those amounts, you're nuts if you make that financial reach and try to beat the game just once. These players know each other. It doesn't mean they'll collude to get your money; they won't have to. They'll most likely eat you alive naturally.

The plan is to talk to this woman for an hour or so, and then I'll go somewhere and watch the game. We start light conversation, and then she tells me the particulars of the cash game, and says she has cleared it with the players—if I'm in town and I want to drop by and watch for a while, I'm welcome to do so. If I write about it, I can't use real names and I can't identify the locale of the game. (NOTE: They had to postpone the game when a couple of the players had to beg off the original date. My window of gambling had closed by the time the game was rescheduled.)

She orders another wine and I get another beer. Three or four guys walk by, and one of them says, "Hope you win your bet with Artie. You're looking good so far."

Somehow, more than two hours have flown by. The Missouri-Memphis game has got to be deep into the first half by now. I excuse myself and head for the nearest men's room, which is on the second floor of the hotel. On the way up, I check my iPhone for the latest updates and learn Missouri is kicking tail. It's 49–36 at the half! (I'll later find out that just before the halftime buzzer, Missouri's Marcus Denmon launched a rocket from three-quarters of the court away—and it hit nothing but net.) With my 4½-point cushion, I'm up by 17½ points. Not quite a lock, but it's going to take a major collapse for me to lose this one.

I never see a single play in the game. The woman and I talk deep into the night. Some of the conversation is about the big-time gamblers she has known, including a guy capable of winning or losing a million dollars in a single weekend at the blackjack tables in Vegas. We talk about people we know whose lives have been seriously fractured by gambling. We talk about relationships that have disintegrated because one party was addicted to the wager. (And it's not always the man who has the gambling problem.) We also talk about some success stories, like the Chicago-area poker player who has won well over a million dollars in tournaments before the age of 25.

We order more drinks, some food, and then one last drink. She tells me what it was like to be a teenager, living in a huge city far from home and modeling for a living. (At that age, I was playing football for Thornridge High School and working part-time in a shoe store.) We talk about our families and some mutual friends, and a few celebrities we both happen to know. We talk about writing and movies and books. For six hours, we talk.

By the time we head into the night, the bartender is putting away the last of the glasses and the staff has wiped down every table but ours.

The Missouri game is long over. I haven't heard an update and I haven't checked my phone since that halftime score, but I've won my bet. I know it. I know it as surely I know this was a great night with an amazing woman—but it's never going to lead to anything because we live in different worlds and we travel in different circles, among other reasons not worth delving into here.

That's OK. Sometimes it's enough to have met someone and to have learned about her world and to have shared a little of your life with her. And then you move on. Ships in the night.

Day 9

**Bankroll:
+$6,980**

"**W**e kind of got punched in the mouth right from the beginning of the game," said Memphis coach John Calipari. "They broke us down defensively like we break people down. They beat us at our own game."

The final score was Missouri 102, Memphis 91. Although Memphis staged a frantic rally late in the game, Mizzou had for all intents and purposes put the game away with a 27–7 run over the last four minutes of the first half and the first four minutes of the second half. The lead was as big as 22 points. At one point late in the game, Memphis cut the lead to 6 (which was still a 10½ point lead as far as I was concerned), but as long as the game didn't head into overtime, I was never in any danger of losing the bet.

With nearly $7,000 in profit so far, I'm starting to believe I can win $20,000 or $30,000 in the first 20 days of the book—and if that happens, maybe I *will* get into that high-stakes cash game. At the very

least I'll double all my minimum bets and see if I can approach six figures in winnings.

That's how it works. I'm up seven grand and I'm already setting my sights on six figures. The gambler is never satisfied. Even when the gambler wins, he or she starts thinking about making a bigger kill in the weeks to come.

Just as it seems like you're not quite playing with real money when you're betting with chips, or you're making a deposit with an online casino using your Amex card, or you're saying "Give me a dime on Missouri" on the phone, the money you win from gambling doesn't seem quite real. For one thing, it's not as if I have $6,980 in cash profits right now sitting in a drawer. I'm up with Sid and he'd be more than happy to get my money to me today, but there's no point in doing that, seeing as how I'm going to continue to place wagers with him over the next three weeks. Same thing with my online accounts at Full Tilt Poker, PokerStars, Bodog, and the other sites. I could cash out, but then I'd just have to deposit the money again so I could keep playing. (Yes, the online sites do make good on their payments. In the summer of 2008, I won nearly $40,000 in tournament play in a little over a month, so I decided to be semi-smart and withdraw a substantial portion of my winnings. I filled out the required forms, and in about 10 business days I received the first of three checks I had requested. It's not exactly fair that they take your money immediately when you lose but they make you wait a couple of weeks to get your winnings, but they do pay. That said, when I see guys winning huge online tournaments and taking home a first prize of $200,000 or more, I think: if I were you I'd get that money out of there as soon as possible. With the ever-shifting nature of legislation regarding online poker, it would seem crazy to leave hundreds of thousands of dollars in some online account managed by an offshore Web company.) And it was just last night that I won the $1,000 bet with Artie Lange. Of course he's good for it, but the guy's dealing with a heroin addiction, so I'm thinking that writing a check to me isn't the first thing on his mind when he struggles out of bed every morning before dawn.

Nevertheless, I know I'm up nearly $7,000, and as always there is the temptation to spend the money on something outside the boundaries of "I need that." One of the most uplifting things about a winning streak is doing something good with the money—helping a friend in need, buying a present for someone just because you want to, donating a healthy portion of the proceeds to a good cause. I've been known to sprain my arm patting myself on the back in public for this or that thing, and I'm sorta doing it again right here, but I'm not going into the details of any charitable donations I'm making during the course of the book, nor am I going to talk about stuff I've done in the past. Let's not kid ourselves—the occasional check to some noble cause hardly makes up for all the time the gambler spends dancing with the devil.

Besides, over the years I've splurged on myself with gambling winnings much more often than I've committed good deeds. I remember a semi-inebriated trip to one of the upscale stores at Caesars Palace in Vegas after I had won several thousand dollars playing blackjack. At the urging of my female companion—who had her eye on a Cartier watch, and that was going to be our next stop—I got fitted for an Armani suit. In the deceptive mirrors of the store, flush with my big run and fueled by multiple beers, I was convinced the suit made me look like George Clooney. I paid $2,000 for it—cash on the nose—and had it sent to my apartment in Chicago.

By the time I got home from Vegas, the blackjack winnings gone and then some, the suit was waiting for me. Sunburned, hung over, and exhausted, I tried it on—and discovered I looked more like an aging George Wendt than George Clooney in his prime. The suit was too small! Either the tailor had screwed up, or I had somehow convinced myself the jacket wasn't too tight when I tried it on.

You want to hear the sound of hearty laughter over the telephone? Call a store in Vegas and tell them you'd like a refund on the tailored suit for which you paid cash.

On another occasion, I used my winnings to buy a Baume & Mercier watch I did not need in the least. At least in this case I was buying

something that wouldn't look stupid once I got back to Chicago. As the owner of the store filled out the paperwork, I noted a sign on the wall above him: Exchanges Only. Absolutely No Refunds.

Understand, this was an upscale store. The cases were filled with gleaming watches bearing brand names like Rolex, Tag Heuer, Omega, Cartier.

"So if I walk out of here with this watch and 10 minutes later I change my mind and ask for a refund, I can't get one?" I said.

He shook his head. "Sorry. I'll give you credit and you can apply it to any watch in the store, but I can't give you your money back."

The owner explained he had to institute the policy because too many customers were coming in and buying $5,000 or $10,000 timepieces—only to ask for a refund later that same day or the next morning.

"They win at blackjack or craps and they want to buy a Rolex. But then they hit a losing streak, or the wife finds out they bought an expensive watch, and they come in the next morning wanting their money back. I'm not a pawn shop."

He mentioned a fairly prominent political name and said this guy had been in the store earlier in the day, eyeing a nice watch. When the politico saw the policy on the wall, he said he'd have to pass. Sure enough, later that night I saw the guy in question, talking up a storm at the craps table as he flung green chips all over the table.

I'm playing in a poker tournament at the Hammond Horseshoe tomorrow and I intend to last deep into the night, so I figure I'll take it easy today and do all my wagering online. (Note: Although I cut back on my schedule a bit during this 30-day run, for the most part I continued with my normal workload. I wanted to see if you could do all this gambling *without* dropping out of the workplace or society. So I continued with my daily column for the *Chicago Sun-Times* and I kept going to daytime and evening screenings of movies while taking meetings about putting a new show on the air. I went on a few dates, had lunches and dinners with friends, attended restaurant openings and charity events, and spent time with my parents, siblings, and nieces and nephews. Of course, there was that one Sunday when I asked my 10-year-old niece and my 8-year-old nephew to pick their favorite colors from a program, and I bet accordingly on the horses with the corresponding colors. I kid you not, one horse came in second and the other finished first.)

I've still got a day or two at the races ahead of me on the calendar, but I figure I'll dip my toes into the horse racing pool by making a few online bets.

I can do one-stop shopping at a site called Youbet.com, where they post the odds, provide handicapping information, and take bets—and they show hundreds of races live every day via streaming video. The video and the audio are surprisingly crisp, and even in an era when we're all jaded by technology, it's pretty amazing to be able to man a computer in Chicago that allows one to place wagers and then watch races taking place in California, Pennsylvania, Florida—even Australia. At one juncture I had a live bet on a race in Australia, and I watched with great amusement as the track officials put a temporary halt on the races due to torrential rains more than nine thousand miles away from my home office. The cameras showed a young couple huddled under an awning, trying to stay dry. How bizarre that gamblers around the globe were suddenly aware of them and what they were doing at that moment.

Once again, though, you're at least another level removed from the betting experience when you bet on the horses online as opposed to making wagers at the track or even the OTB. Instead of marking your program and then heading over to the teller or the machine, where you exchange real money for tickets, you simply make a deposit from your checking account or your credit card, and you place bets with a click of the mouse. Every time I'm about to put $50 on a horse to win, I'm tempted to hit the "Delete" button on that bet and make it $100. Why bet a little when you can bet a little more? It's all so damn convenient.

I bet on races at Philadelphia Park and Beulah, Woodbine and Monticello, Mountaineer and Yonkers. Thanks to the video component, I can see if it's raining in the East or sunny in California. I can hear the local announcers talking about why the odds have plummeted on a particular horse, or how a certain jockey is having a huge day. Sometimes I make a bet based on a jockey or trainer, or a speed rating, or some other semilogical factor. Often it's because I like the name and/or the odds. Usually I don't like betting the favorites or extreme long shots; I prefer to find a horse I like at 8-1 or 14-1. At least then I have a realistic shot.

While I'm betting on the races, I log onto to Full Tilt Poker and deposit $500 in my account. I'm not interested in playing a long tournament today. In fact, I don't even have the patience for a "sit 'n' go," i.e., a one-table tournament where you have nine players and the top two or three get paid.

Today I'm going to play heads-up. Just me, one on one against some guy from down the block or from halfway around the world, with a wacky nickname and a cartoon avatar. All I have to do is register for a heads-up game at the denomination of my choosing—and usually within seconds, somebody else signs up to take me on. I've played against men and women who were sitting at their computers in Hong Kong, the Netherlands, Paris, Rome, the Philippines, you name it. I've also found myself playing opponents who were no more than a mile from my house.

I start off playing a $115 buy-in game. Each player starts with the same amount of chips and you keep going until one player has all the chips. Sometimes that takes one or two hands; sometimes it takes a half hour.

The first game takes three hands. On the third hand, my opponent gets a pair of Queens and raises, I have Ace-King and reraise, he goes all-in, I call. I get an Ace on the flop to take the lead and it holds, and that's that. In about two minutes, my $115 has been turned into $230.

So I move up and play in a $230 heads-up game, and after I win four out of six, I move up again, to a $345 game.

(In the meantime, I'm keeping tabs on the action at a dozen race-tracks. I've hit one small winner in the first 10 races. I switch gears and bet a couple of favorites, including a 7-5 shot in a fucking harness race. The favorites finish far back.)

Another heads-up win, and I move up again. Now I'm playing for $570 per game.

With those stakes, I can be sure of one thing: my opponent is going to have far more experience playing at this level than I have. Although I've been playing online poker for a number of years, I usually confine my play to the big tournaments, where you pay an entry fee of a couple hundred dollars and you have a shot at winning enough to buy a car and in some cases enough to buy a condo. Relatively low risk, high reward—and I gain a ton of experience.

When you start playing in cash games online, especially at the higher stakes, you have to understand that thousands of people—most of the individuals at your table—are doing this for a living. They are perched at their computers for 10, 12, 14 hours a day, grinding it out. They live for the moments when an inexperienced player sits down with a bankroll of several thousand dollars, looking to make a quick kill.

So it is in the heads-up world. If you want to play for $570 a game—or $1,080, or $2,100, or $5,100—you'll find action. (As I write this, a player named "skilled_sox1" is sitting at a $1,000 table at Full Tilt, waiting for a heads-up opponent to take him on.)

My first opponent is a maniac that raises every hand. Literally every hand. This type of aggression is commonplace online, especially in the high-stakes matches. You have to be willing to make bluffs of your own, coming over the top with nothing in your hand, or you'll be steamrolled. I'm down by a chip count of $1,800 to $1,200 before I can even catch my breath and start fighting back. The great thing about going against these super-aggressive guys is they'll often call as quickly as they raise. Since they're lying most of the time, they figure you're bluffing as well. If you catch a big hand and they have even bottom pair, they might call you all the way down.

That's what happens with this guy. I get a flush on the turn and bet big, and he calls. I bet the pot on the river, and he calls—with nothing but a pair of 9s. Now he's short-stacked and he starts going all-in with every hand, and I patiently wait until I get a nice A-J against his Q-10. He hits nothing but air on the flop, the turn, and the river, and my superior hand holds up.

Boom! Game over.

The same player accepts a rematch and we go at it again.

And four more times after that.

He wins four of the five matches. Son of a bitch keeps calling my bluffs and bluffing me off pots. When I call him down, he usually has the better hand.

In other words, he's outplaying me.

I take a small break to concentrate on the races and to make a few bets on the NBA. Then it's back to the Full Tilt tables, where I play a number of games at the $335 and $570 level. After a decent run in some $570 games—enough to get me within shouting distance of breaking even—I decide to play a match for $1,070. A guy with the handle of "369 TBAGS" sits across from me. Maybe he's a patriot and a historian. Maybe he's into something kinky. I don't ask.

On the very first hand, he raises. I have a pair of Queens, so I come back with a hefty reraise. He immediately shoves all-in.

Jesus. The only two hands in the entire spectrum that beat me are A-A and K-K. I could see folding Q-Q at the final table of the World Series of Poker if you felt certain your opponent had the best hand—but heads-up? If you fold Q-Q in this situation, you shouldn't be playing at all.

I call, and he turns over Ace-King unsuited.

In heads-up poker, the A-K unsuited is strong, but it's only the 12th-best starting hand. When you see Q-Q against A-K heads-up on TV, the commentators and the players will often refer to it as "a classic race," meaning the hands are essentially equal in value before we see the next five cards, and it's a sprint to see who will wind up with the best hand. That's not really true. In this case a pair of Queens is a 56 to 42 percent favorite over A-K, with a 2 percent chance of a tie. In politics, that's pretty close to a landslide.

With the turn of a single card, I lose $1,000 in a heads-up poker match on Full Tilt.

The flop comes 4 of spades, 6 of diamonds, 5 of spades. I am now a 67 to 27 percent favorite to take down this game. Ol' Teabags has to be rooting for a tie at this point. For example, if the next two cards are a 7 and an 8, we'll both have a straight.

Here comes the turn card. It's the King of diamonds.

Such bullshit.

I'm screwed. With that one card, I go from being a heavy favorite to a huge underdog. I have a 5 percent chance of winning, as the remaining Queens are the only two cards in the deck that will give me a better hand. They call that a "two-outer," and it happens more on TV than it happens in real life because they show only the most dramatic hands on television.

The river card is a useless 4, giving my opponent the victory. With a sickening sound effect, all the "chips" are shuffled over to the other guy, who types the obligatory *gg* (for "good game") and disappears from the felt.

That's it. In one hand, I lost a cool $1,070. I turn away from the Full Tilt table just in time to see the stretch run at the latest race at Oaklawn.

As the winner crosses the finish line, my horse isn't even in the picture.

Day 10

Bankroll:
+$4,550

Early morning. The calendar says it's spring, but the snow whirling outside the window says it's still winter in Chicago.

I try not to think too much about my online losses on the ponies and the pocket Queens as I roust myself out of bed, throw on sweats, and make my way to the East Bank Club gym, which is already bustling with activity on this weekend morning. Fueled by the sounds of Linkin Park, U2, Coldplay, and the soundtrack to *Rent*—and, yes, I'm secure enough in my heterosexuality to admit I often run to the sounds of *Rent*—I get in a four-mile run/walk and hit the weights for a half hour or so.

Why am I lifting weights at this point in my life? I'm not really sure. It's not as if anyone is going to ask me to help move their refrigerator any time soon. The only thing I'll be lifting in the near future is a finger or someone's spirits.

But I proceed with the routine, because when it comes to working out, I'm still a basic run-and-lift kind of guy. I recognize the benefits of yoga and I salute those who do Pilates, but other than some martial arts classes here and there, I like to stick with the basic exercise groups: running, walking, lifting weights, playing 12-inch softball, maybe a little pickup basketball.

I've been trying hard to maintain a somewhat-healthy lifestyle during the course of the 30-day adventure. Eating more chicken and vegetables than pizza and red meat, working out four or five times a week, imbibing in moderation.

So far I'm batting about .250.

The gambler's way is not conducive to good health. You spend endless hours in sedentary mode, hunched over a slot machine or a blackjack table, surrounded by smokers at the craps table, stressing over your bets while taking in the games at a sports bar. During the so-called dinner breaks at poker tournaments, about half the players spend the hour smoking cigarettes, bitching about their bad beats, downing drinks, and calling their friends to see if there's a good cash game anywhere. Then they shovel down a cheeseburger and return to the table.

Granted, some of the younger players on the poker circuit are all about the workout and the vegetarian meals. But visit any poker room—or, for that matter, any casino in America—and you'll see an awful lot of people who look like they haven't seen the inside of a gym since high school. And even then, they were having a helluva time climbing that damn rope.

I've tried to buck that trend on occasion. On some trips to Vegas, I'll pack an extra bag filled with workout clothes, knowing I'll feel like an idiot if I return home without having even opened that bag. If I bring the gym shoes, etc., I'll force myself to hit the gym in the hotel, if only to run a couple of miles and sweat out the drinks from the night before.

In that same vein, I don't always drink when I'm gambling, especially if I'm in a two-day poker tournament—but let's face it, when

I'm at the blackjack table or the slots and a waitress comes by with the call of "Cocktails!" I'm like the majority of gamblers. I'll order a drink.

Some gamblers ingest other things to keep them up or to help them sleep. Some go to very dark places after a thrilling winning streak or a devastating run of bad luck. Suffice it to say that if I were to visit those places during this run, I would not be unfamiliar with them. But I'm doing my best to stay away from the truly dark stuff. That was another life.

Seeing as how I'm undertaking a *Super Size Me* type of experiment, substituting a daily diet of gambling for a daily diet of fast food, I figured I'd try to actually lose weight over the course of this month. Sure enough, I'm down a few pounds, but I can guarantee you I'm not losing the weight via any method you'll ever see advertised on TV or in the magazines. Half the time it's because I've been gambling all day and I forgot to eat another meal after breakfast.

Today I'm trying to get back on the right track. After the good, strong workout, I head home through the still-swirling snow, park the car in my garage, and walk over to Tempo Cafe to meet a friend for breakfast. A healthful breakfast, dammit. Keep the eggs and sausage away from me.

She knows about the gambling experiment. Everybody in my life knows about my gambling experiment.

"So are you winning so far?" she asks as I pour coffee for both of us. (Hey, I ain't giving up caffeine until the day a doctor tells me if I have one more cup of coffee it'll kill me.) This is the question everyone asks me. Among nongamblers, the thought seems to be if I don't show a sizable profit at the end of the 30 days, the book will be a chronicle of "failure." They tend to think of it as more of a "how to win" guide than a rollercoaster ride through more than a dozen different types of gambling. If I were to write a how-to book, I wouldn't be risking thousands of dollars on Michigan lottery tickets and fucking baccarat.

"I can't really talk about it until the book comes out," I say. There's no law or even an agreement with the publisher stating

I'm strictly forbidden from delving into the details of the adventure—but obviously I don't want to give away too much during the adventure. After my appearance on *Howard Stern*, I heard from more than a dozen radio, TV, and print outlets requesting interviews—but I politely declined, saying I'd rather concentrate on the gambling for now. I can talk about the gambling when it's all said and I'm done.

I explain the premise of the book to my friend, who is so wholesome that people sometimes think she's putting them on. She's like Bryce Dallas Howard with less of an edge. She's also a terrific listener, and she loves the premise of the book, even if she doesn't know the difference between a double down and a pocket pair.

"So you've been thinking about doing this book for years, is that right?" she says.

Indeed. I just needed the right window of time to make it happen.

"OK. So were you more interested in doing this book because you're fascinating by the gambling culture, or because you wanted to explore your own gambling problem?"

My what?

"Your gambling problem."

"Is it a problem?" I ask. "I'm not so sure it's a problem. I've always thought of it as . . . I don't know. A particularly intense hobby."

"All right," she says. "You know more about all this than I do."

That's right, I do. Gambling problem? Who's got a problem? And can you please finish your egg-white omelet with no cheese but extra broccoli so I can get to my poker tournament?

We linger over coffee a bit, talking about nongambling things. Family members, upcoming events, the flippin' economy. For the most part I'm not even thinking about the poker tournament that awaits me. For the most part.

By the time we head out, pausing to grab a couple of mints at the register, the snow has started to subside. Looks like the drive to northwest Indiana won't be a problem.

By noon, I'm taking my seat in the poker room at the Hammond Horseshoe, arguably the best-looking and the best-run casino in the Midwest. When you park your car in their lot, you're well aware of the industrial surroundings and the less-than-glamorous neighborhood. But once you set foot inside the casino, it feels as if you're in a legitimate gaming emporium that wouldn't be out of place on the Strip. After a recent $500 million expansion and renovation, the Horseshoe boasts some 3,200 slot machines, nearly 100 gaming tables, and the largest poker room in the Midwest. The 350,000-square-foot casino's ceiling is more than 20 feet high, framed with ornate columns and decorated with gold- and silver-leaf grillwork, as well as dozens of works of original art. Entertainers such as Jay Leno and Melissa Etheridge play the 3,000-seat Venue, which has also been the host for some of the largest circuit events in the history of the World Series of Poker. We are a long way from the Midwest riverboat casinos of the early 1990s—boats that would actually leave dock and sail down the river for 90 minutes or so while you played $5-limit blackjack.

Today's tournament is in the poker room, which rivals the Bellagio's for size and style. In addition to the tourney, there are dozens of cash games in full swing. The last time I was here was after midnight on a Friday; there wasn't a single seat available.

The buy-in is $1,560, and we've got one hundred entrants and counting. The top 10 percent will be paid. First place will be worth more than $41,000.

My table is in a far corner of the poker room. There are two flat-screen monitors nearby. One is showing the latest NCAA action. The other has all the details on this tournament: number of entrants, players remaining in the tournament, average chip stack, information on the antes and the blinds and when they'll next go up. Over the course of a tourney, you can't help but check the monitor every few minutes. It's an invaluable source of information that will help you make key decisions, like whether or not to make a standard raise or go all-in. (If

your stack is well below average and the blinds and antes are about to go up yet again, what are you waiting for? Get all your chips in there ASAP!)

The dealer says hello and asks about the recently released movie *Watchmen*. Any good? Faithful to the graphic novel? Sigh. OK. We're going to talk movies today. Sometimes I can play for six hours without anyone asking me about a movie. Sometimes it happens within the first 20 seconds. Inevitably the questions are about the next *Iron Man* movie or the most recent installment of the *Batman* franchise. Once in a while someone will ask me about a foreign film. (It's usually someone for whom the movie is not foreign; it's from their homeland.) Nobody ever asks what I thought of *The Sisterhood of the Traveling Pants 2* or *He's Just Not That Into You*.

A couple of years ago I was playing in the Sunday tournament at the Bellagio. By happenstance, I wound up at a table with James Woods and Montel Williams, two of the better celebrity poker players. Woods was as friendly as can be with all the players—he even offered to buy lunch for everyone at the table—but at least three hours went by before either one of us talked shop. Finally, during a 10-minute break, I shook his hand and told him I'd interviewed him in L.A. once and we had wound up ordering apple pie from room service. As if that would mean anything to him. Woods told me he spent the first hour at the table trying to figure out if I had done a movie with him at some point. Then when he realized it was me, he was trying to recall if I'd been good to him in my reviews over the years. For the record: almost any movie is better with Jimmy Woods in it.

Today we have a friendly table, for the most part. All guys, ranging in age from early 20s to late 50s. Whites, blacks, Asians. Many seem to know each other. In fact as I look about the room, it appears as if the majority of the players in this tournament have tangled with each other before. There's a lot of good-natured heckling back and forth, and at least one "last longer" bet among a large group of participants. Heck, I'm not even a semiregular at these Midwestern tourneys, and I recognize at least 15 faces from previous events.

The one jerkoff at my table is the guy to my immediate right. He's the kind of player who says, "I'm going to let you have this one," just before he folds, as if he knows his hand is better but he's going to do you a favor and let you win.

Jerkoff is wearing sunglasses and headphones, the music so loud it's bleeding through. Every once in a while when someone at the end of the table makes a raise and the action comes his way, he takes off the sunglasses, removes the headphones, leans over the table, and says, "Is that a raise?"

Playing in a tournament at the Hammond Horseshoe Casino.

And then the dealer has to patiently repeat what everyone at the table has already heard: yes, it's a raise. Here's an idea, buddy: you'll be able to see and hear a lot better if you *take off the headphones and the sunglasses.*

Early in the tournament, the button raises him for the second time in a row, and he folds, saying, "The next time you do that, I'll knock you out. I'll know your cards right down to the suits." OK, tough guy.

You wonder: did the poker craze and all the trash-talking on TV turn this guy into an asshole, or was he an asshole who was attracted to the poker craze because it allows him to play up his obnoxious his personality?

I'm guessing it was the latter.

About two hours into the tournament, I get pocket 5s in early position and I raise about four times the big blind.

Two players call me. These days it's almost impossible to make a bet big enough to take the pot down before the flop. Somebody's always calling. Somebody's always thinking their 6-4 is only a 38 percent underdog, and if they catch the right cards they'll win a big pot.

The flop comes King-Ace-King. Not good for my small pair. Surely one of the two other players has an Ace or maybe even a King. But I make the standard continuation bet, representing that I'm the one with the big hand. Maybe I'm up against something like A-10 and a pair of 9s and they'll fold. Probably not, but maybe.

The first player folds, but the guy in the big blind raises me. It's not much of a raise, meaning he's either got a ridiculously huge hand and he's trying to reel me in, or he's somewhere in between and he's trying to figure out if I whiffed altogether with that flop.

I make the call. Too many chips in there to fold, but I don't want to risk my tournament life with a re-raise.

The turn card is a glorious five. Unless he's got A-A or A-K, I've got him.

I check. He bets about half the pot. I go a little Hollywood, as if I have something like Ace-Queen or pocket 10s and I'm lamenting my fate. In reality, I'm thinking he has something like K-10 or K-J, giving him a set and a straight draw, and he's positive he's got the best hand.

"I'm all-in," I say, and he cries, "Call!" before I can even touch my chips.

As quickly as possible, I turn over my 5-5 to reveal the full house. I hate it when players hang onto their cards, waiting for the other guy to show first. It's not going to change your fate, and it makes you look like jerk.

In the meantime, he's triumphantly turning over his K-10, but his glee disappears when he sees I got lucky on the turn. Now the only way he can beat me is with a King for four Kings, or an Ace or a 10 for a bigger full house than mine.

The river is an 8, and he's gone. To his credit, he shakes my hand and says, "Nice hand," neglecting to mention that he was *way* ahead until I spiked that 5 on the turn. As the cliche goes, that's poker.

We're nearing the second break of the day and the field has been narrowed to about 70. I've got well above the average stack size, and I see no reason why I can't handle this field and make the final table, where anything can happen.

Poker face.

Seems like I always have trouble with the middle rounds of these tournaments. I go card-dead, and when I try to make a move, somebody calls me.

That's certainly the pattern today. For the last two hours, I've seen exactly one premium starting hand—a pair of Queens. I made a big raise, got called by one player, bet again after the flop, and he folded and asked me how the book was coming along. He's the third player today who either heard me on *Stern* or saw an item in the *Sun-Times* about the book.

I'm getting restless. I'm watching my chip stack dwindle to about average size. Just outside the poker room, the casino is bursting with action. Maybe I should be out there doing that group roulette thing or trying my luck at the slots.

The player to my left requests a towel. He's taken off his sweatshirt because it's rather warm in here, but he doesn't want to put his bare forearms on the padded cushion surrounding our table. "You get sick from all the germs," he explains to me.

OK. But what about those chips everyone is fondling at all times? And the cards that pass from player to player? Might they be carrying even more potential viruses than the cushion?

Action comes around to me and I limp in with 8-7 off-suit. Four players limp in as well.

The flop comes 6-6-5. Hey, that's a straight draw for me. Of course, somebody could have pocket 5s like I had early in the tournament, in which case I'd be nearly dead, but you can't think that way. After three players check, I make a pot-sized bet. An expressionless guy wearing designer shades hesitates, and then calls. One other player calls. Everyone else folds.

The turn is a 3. We all put on the brakes and check.

The river is a 9. There's no flush out there, and the board is now: 6-6-5-3-9.

Unless someone has a full house, and I doubt someone has a full house, that's a great river card for me. I've got the nut straight.

I make a bet, maybe one-third the pot. I want to get called if someone has a set of 6s or two pair.

One player folds. The guy in the designer shades waits, and waits, and waits—and raises the absolute minimum amount.

Huh? This should make me put on the brakes. Instead, I quickly come to the conclusion that he flopped a set and he thinks I have either a big overpair or I'm making a bluff. There's no way he can figure I limped in from early position with 8-7 off-suit, especially given my conservative table image. Besides, I've committed well over 50 percent of my chips to this pot and I've got him covered, so why not just raise a few thousand more?

"Reraise," I say.

"All-in," he replies.

Shit. What just happened? Now I'm pretty sure I'm beat, but I have to call.

He flips over his cards without changing expression.

I was right about him not having the full house. He doesn't have a full house or a set—he has four of a kind.

The guy had a pair of 6s in his hand. He had flopped quads. He had the nuts from the start. If I'd missed my straight draw, I'd have gotten out of there with minimum damage. Instead, I'm forced to show my suddenly impotent straight while everyone at the table whistles and chuckles at the sight of the quads.

"Nice hand," I say weakly, as most of my chips make their way across the table.

He just nods—just barely nods to the point where I'm not even sure if he nods—from behind his shades, which I find incredibly infuriating. Oh, you're so fucking cool when you flop four of a kind. You're Phil Fucking Ivey, pal. I bow to your coolness and your greatness.

Only later do I realize he had never removed his Bose headphones and he probably never even heard me.

I hang around for a few more hours, getting pocket Queens twice more but never doubling up, and the blinds and antes start to eat away at my chip stack. Finally I move all-in with King-10.

An Asian guy in a skin-tight black T-shirt is in the big blind. Everyone else has folded, and I'd be perfectly happy to just take down the blinds and antes, but he calls.

And then he looks at me and waits for me to turn over my cards. All right, no problem. I show him the K-10. He smiles and turns over a pair of Aces.

"Really?" I say. "You were waiting to see what I have? You don't just show me the courtesy of letting me know you've got pocket Aces? That's great. Kind of a dick move."

He doesn't care. He just smiles again and says, "Nothing personal." In my experience, when someone says, "Nothing personal," it's the same as when they say, "It's not about the money." Sure it is.

After the turn, I'm drawing dead. The 10 on the river doesn't mean anything against his Aces. I shake hands with everyone, including the guy who knocked me out, and head out to the casino with steam coming out of my ears.

Any time you're knocked out of a tournament, you immediately start replaying hands in your head and bemoaning your bad luck. I

can honestly say that at least 75 percent of the time when I'm eliminated from a tourney, I made my biggest play when I had the best
hand going in. If you get beat on the draw, God bless.

This time, though, I did most of the damage to myself. The fatal
hand for me wasn't the K-10 against the pocket Aces; it was the straight
against the quads. Had I not been so greedy, had I just called on the
river when I had the chance, I would have been in good enough shape
to make at least one more serious run. But I chopped myself off at the
knees, and now I'm out of the smoke-free environment of the poker
room and into the raucous madness of the main gaming floor.

I stop to play a few blackjack hands and lose six in a row. My saving grace for the day is the NCAA tournament, where I pick up a net
of a few hundred in profits. It even works to my advantage when I
can't get a signal from the casino as I'm trying to make a bet on the
North Carolina game. By the time I make my way outside and try to
place the wager, the game is underway and it's too late. I would have
lost that bet, so I saved $400 by not getting a phone connection when
I needed it.

Days 11–14

**Bankroll:
+$3,990**

The Illinois Senate has approved a measure legalizing gambling machines in taverns and truck stops across the state.

Video poker was once labeled "the crack cocaine of gambling" by former governor Rod Blagojevich, before Blago himself became the crack cocaine of late-night monologue writers.

Cook County sheriff Tom Dart was vehemently opposed to the bill.

"What a mistake," said Dart. "This is a horrible idea because this is a form of gambling that by its very nature is very addictive. You are going to have guys dropping their whole paycheck at the bar."

It's hard to argue with Dart. If the Illinois House of Representatives and Governor Patrick Quinn approve this proposal and it becomes law, it will signal the beginning of a horrific journey for more than a handful of gamblers. We will be hearing stories about men and

women losing their jobs, their families, everything, because of their addiction to video poker.

The main concern with video gambling machines is making sure there's a reasonable payout. How is the state going to regulate thousands of machines to make sure they haven't been tampered with to give the house an insane edge?

Then again, even the tightest video gambling machines don't rake in percentages comparable to what the state gets with the lottery or even horse racing.

I'm in the running for a house in San Diego, a 2009 Corvette, a weekend in Miami, a year's worth of pet food, a trip to Broadway, a diamond necklace, a new pair of shoes every week for a year, and $10,000 in restaurant gift certificates, among other prizes.

"Eat your weight in cash!" is the tease for the dining-out sweepstakes. For a minute there I thought they were saying I was going to have to eat 185 pounds of cash, but what they really mean is you'll get a certain amount of money based on your weight, and that money will be delivered in the form of restaurant cards. Of course, if you go out to eat that often you'll probably wind up weighing more than you did when you won the contest.

Every day in this country, you can enter hundreds if not thousands of sweepstakes and raffles. The difference between a sweepstakes and a raffle? The first carries the "No purchase necessary" stipulation. You fill out the form and you're one of eight kabillion hopefuls. With a raffle, you're buying a ticket and usually there are a limited number of entries, thus giving something approaching a decent chance of actually winning.

I've entered myself (and if you've ever entered yourself, you know how painful that can be—*ba-dum-bum*) in about 25 sweepstakes, and I buy in for 6 or 7 raffles. For $150, I have a ticket for the Dream House Raffle to benefit Ronald McDonald House Charities of San

Diego. The grand prize is a $1.95 million house in San Diego—or $1.6 million in cash. Second prize is $25,000. Little bit of a drop-off there.

After I announced the book project, I heard from dozens of individuals and organizations inviting me to play bingo, participate in charity poker tournaments, join a fantasy league, etc. One offer was from a woman in the southwest suburbs of Chicago, who wrote:

> I have a great suggestion for your gambling challenge. . . .
>
> For $1,000 you can purchase 20 raffle tickets at $50 apiece for our "Be There 4 Bill" benefit to be held in Merrionette Park. There will be one $10,000 winner, one $5,000 winner and 10 winners of $1,000, based on a maximum of 1,000 tickets sold.
>
> By purchasing 20 tickets, you will have 2 percent of the total available tickets in your possession. If by chance one of your stubs is not drawn, you will still be a WINNER for donating to this cause.
>
> The benefit is in honor of Bill Pranske, a lifelong Mount Greenwood resident who was diagnosed with inoperable cancer in March 2008. The Be There 4 Bill committee was formed to help defray medical costs and extra expenses Bill and his family have endured over the past year.
>
> Unfortunately, Bill passed away on Feb. 15, 2009. . . .

I visit the Web site and learn that Bill Pranske was 52 years old. There's a photo of a smiling man with a friendly face, along with his lovely wife and three beautiful daughters. Until five minutes ago, I'd never heard of Bill. Now I feel just terrible for his family, and wonder what kind of higher power allows such pain and suffering to enter so many lives every day.

I write a check for $1,000 and send it to the committee.

Other end of the spectrum. In perhaps the silliest gambling adventure to date, I sit in an Irish pub with a gambling friend and we flip a coin one hundred times for $100 a pop.

Well. We don't flip a real coin. We don't want to look like a couple of idiots in a bar flipping a silver dollar and yelling "Heads!" or "Tails!" Instead, we're a couple of idiots in a bar hunched over the coin-flip application on my iPhone, which allows you to pick the quarter of any state. For no reason, I go with an Alaskan quarter. The tails side features a bear with a fish in its mouth and the phrase "The Great Land." You tap the virtual quarter, and it flies "up" and lands with a realistic sound effect. Now we don't have to worry about a coin bouncing off the table or landing in my glass of Stella Artois.

We've agreed that he'll call the first 50 flips and I'll call the second 50 flips.

The first toss comes up heads, followed by tails, tails, tails, tails, and tails.

Question: if you were calling the next flip, would you go with heads or tails? After five flips in a row were tails, is the next flip more likely to be heads?

We all know the heads/tails percentage is precisely 50-50. (Unless the coin lands on its edge, which isn't an option with the iPhone app.) So when you see tails five times in a row, there's a natural tendency to believe heads is "due," to "even things out."

The problem with that line of thinking is we're projecting our feelings onto an object that has no thought process or memory. The coin doesn't know it's due to come up heads. For that matter, the dice don't know they're due to hit a hard 10, nor does the slot machine know it's due to yield a big payout. Each flip of the coin or roll of the dice is an independent occurrence, not in the least bit influenced by the previous flip or roll, or the next flip or roll. Yes, over the infinite long run, a coin should land on heads 50 percent of the time and on tails 50 percent of the time. But if you flipped a coin 1 million times, a) your thumb might fall off, and b) you might see the coin land on tails 700,000 times and heads 300,000 times—and those figures would have absolutely no bearing on the next million flips.

Even when you're playing roulette in a casino, you can make your bets electronically.

Gamblers have an intellectual understanding of this, but we persist in believing in "hot streaks" at craps and "cold numbers" at the roulette wheel. (Most modern roulette games have an electronic board with state-of-the-art graphics informing players of the five "hottest" numbers and the five "coldest" numbers. They'll tell you the exact percentage of spins in the current session that came up black and the percentage that came up red. This is all pure hype and superstition. If the number 23 comes up three times in a row, the odds of it coming up on the next spin are the same as they are for every other number on the wheel.)

Over the course of 100 flips, tails comes up 58 times and heads up comes up 42 times. My buddy winds up with 53 victories to my 47. I count out $600 in cash, order another round, and tell the waitress, "He'll be taking care of the check."

I'm in the car, listening to the *Stern* show, when the subject of my bet with Artie Lange comes up. Lange informs Howard he lost the bet to me.

Howard laughs and warns his audience, "Don't gamble with Richard Roeper."

What he doesn't know is that I've been struggling over these last few days, whether it's losing $600 on coin flips, betting into quads at the poker table, or trying my luck in some online cash games and tournaments and falling short. The only thing that's saving me is my

continued success rate with the NCAA tournament. My winning percentage is well over 60 percent. Now *there's* a streak that's bound to cool off soon.

On Day 14 of the adventure I'm going to the dogs. Literally.

It's about a 60-mile drive from downtown Chicago to the Dairyland Greyhound Park in Kenosha, Wisconsin. On this brisk but sunny day, I'm blasting the 1980s station on satellite radio with the windows rolled down, zooming up I-94 at a pace just slightly faster than the (ahem) legal speed limit and pitying all the suckers who are working today. I mean, I'm working, but my "day at the office" today consists of a relaxing drive into Wisconsin, where I can risk real money on a bunch of dogs racing around an oval. I've had real jobs. This ain't one of 'em.

In fact, I've been on a professional lucky streak for nearly my entire career—something I try to remember always. Sometimes I get irritated when people say, "Must be nice to watch movies for a living," or, "So you just get to write about whatever you write about?" I want to sit down with these people and tell them about all the hours I put in doing behind-the-scenes work. I want to invite them to watch crappy movie after crappy movie in a dark screening room in the middle of the day. I'd like to explain to them the challenge isn't writing *a* column, it's writing a column every day, four or five times a week, for 20 years. I'd like to make them understand that between the column and the blog and the Twittering and the Facebooking, the book projects and the TV show I'm trying to put together, the meetings and the screenings and the appearances and the speeches and the guest shots on radio and TV, it feels like I'm never *not* working.

And then I realize I should shut the fuck up.

The scene I always quote from *Broadcast News* is the exchange between William Hurt's handsome/nice/lucky anchor and Albert Brooks's not-so-handsome/not-always-nice/not-so-lucky reporter.

"What happens when your real life exceeds your dreams?" says Hurt.

"You *keep it to yourself*," hisses Brooks.

Exactly.

I remember watching the early evening news in Chicago one night when there was a gigantic Powerball drawing coming up later. The obligatory feature report showed folks lining up to buy their tickets, talking about their relatively modest dreams if they should win. ("I'm going to pay off all my bills"; "I'm going to get a new car." Folks, it's $135 million—you'll be able to do more than wipe out your Master-Card balance and buy a new Toyota). Back in the studio, there was a bit of happy talk about the lottery, and one of the anchors mentioned he had bought his tickets and he was hoping to hit it big, and I thought, *You stupid schmuck, you're reading the news on TV for a half million dollars a year. You've already hit it big in the Life Lottery. Don't insult the viewer by pretending you're just like him, dreaming your ship will come in one day.*

Finding a parking spot at Dairyland Greyhound Park isn't much of a challenge. It's about 15 percent occupied, at the most. There's a real bite to the winds whipping across the open lot, but I'll be in the large, enclosed grandstand area.

I take the escalator to the second floor and enter an area that resembles a VFW hall crossed with a sports bar. It's a clean, quiet space with pockets of bettors scattered about, sitting at the tables or the bar, poring over their programs before making their next pick. The crowd is mostly middle-aged white males. A few couples. Some senior citizens.

It's seven minutes to post time for the second race. I've got my program and I've got a wad of cash—and I have almost zero knowledge of greyhound racing. I've been to the dog track only once before in my life, when I was about 18 and I was on vacation in Florida. The only thing I remember about that trip was that my grandmother tried to take a picture with a flash camera, and an employee told her that was forbidden because it might spook the dogs. And oh yeah—I had about $40 in my pocket when I went to the track, and about no dollars in my pocket when we left.

Before we get into my Dairyland betting adventures, a few words about the incendiary topic of animal cruelty and the sport of racing, whether it's dogs or horses. I know a few people in the horse racing game, and though I'm not going to profess any expertise on how the horses are treated overall, I can tell you these folks love horses like parents love their children. They take great care of these animals. I don't personally know anyone in the greyhound game, but I did talk to a couple of people in the industry while prepping the book, and they seemed to have the same level of concern and affection for their dogs.

I know some of you are rolling your eyes right now, amazed at my naivete. You're getting ready to send me links to YouTube videos showing examples of shocking abuse. When I mentioned in my blog I was going to spend a day at the dog track, I heard from a number of readers expressing sadness and even outrage that I'd patronize the sport.

From Todd S:
Hey Richard!
I am a big fan. I just wanted to let you know about the cruelties of dog racing. The dogs are put in cages for 20 hours a day while sitting on shredded paper. They are fed rancid meat most of the time and most injuries occurred on the track are not treated correctly. I adopted a greyhound with a broken foot, that didn't heal right. The dogs do not receive the appropriate dental care. After racing my dog had to have 11 teeth removed because of her poor diet. Dog racing isn't something that should be glamorized or encouraged.

From Kristin70:

Richard: I am really, really disappointed. I have read your works for years and I was a huge fan of your style and ideas. Please take one hour and educate yourself on dog racing. Do the dogs love to run? Perhaps. But at what cost? Due to their size, ease of transportation and ease of disposal, inhumane treatment is rampant. Not all owners treat them badly, of course. But the numbers of those who do cannot be ignored. I do not own greyhounds, have never attended a race, but the credible documentation from both private and government sectors is available to anyone who makes the effort to find it. Yes, as of now, you have the right to make the choice to attend the races just as your readers can choose to read your works or not. I feel strongly enough about this subject and particularly, your choice to promote it that I can no longer follow your career.

I hope Kristin70 has reconsidered her decision. If I stopped reading, watching, and listening to everyone with whom I disagreed with on some issue, my worldview would be considerably narrowed.

You can find dozens of Web sites and articles lambasting greyhound racing as a cruel enterprise—and just as many sites and articles defending the industry and countering the alleged propaganda from the other side.

From the Humane Society of the United States: "Racing greyhounds spend the majority of their adult lives in crates or pens or in forced enclosures. Human companionship is limited. Many enclosures are not climate-controlled. . . ."

From the Greyhound Lovers League: "At the kennels, greyhounds are let outside to relieve themselves and play for about a half hour, four to six times a day. . . . Dogs are basically lounging animals. Once they reach maturity, pet dogs spend the vast majority of their time lying around the house. A greyhound's crate is his bed."

The anti–greyhound racing movement often claims the industry uses "bait animals," including live rabbits, to train greyhounds, and

that these animals are routinely maimed and killed. The Greyhound Lovers League counters, "Live lure training is illegal in 49 states, and any trainer caught using live lures is banned from racing. And who would teach the rabbit to run around the track?"

(The Dairyland Greyhound Park has had its issues. In December 2008, Don Walker of the *Milwaukee Journal-Sentinel* reported, "A total of three greyhounds broke their legs last Saturday, and several trainers and other kennel workers complained that the surface of the track was too hard. While racing was not halted on Saturday, some races were delayed because of concerns about the condition of the track.")

Although I'm all for the humane treatment of animals and I cringe every time a racehorse has to be put down, I can't say I've spent a whole lot of time, or any time at all, campaigning for the end of greyhound racing as we know it. Of course I hope these dogs are treated well, but I'm at the dog track today because I'm exploring as many gambling options as possible over the 30-day trip, and though greyhound racing represents a tiny fraction of the billions of dollars wagered in this country every year, it still exists in about 15 states.

That said, there are few things more depressing in this world than seeing a 30ish man with a little boy of about five at the friggin' dog track in Wisconsin on a weekday afternoon. The little guy is bounding about, looking for something to keep him amused, while dad drinks a beer and marks his program. I'm imagining the scenario: Dad picks up his son on visitation day and says, "You want to go see some doggies?" and the son eagerly says, "Sure!" Dad adds, "Just don't tell Mommy we went to the dog zoo again." There's no way of knowing the actual scenario, because when I approach Dad or Uncle Joe or whoever the heck he is and ask if I can talk to him for a book I'm writing, he reacts as if I've just told him I'd like the keys to his car.

It's just a minute before race #2 goes off. I put $30 to win and $50 to place on the #5 horse—er, dog—and I go with a quinella on #5 and #7, meaning that as with an exacta box, I need those two dogs to finish first and second, regardless of order.* The #5 dog, Hundred, apparently has raced three times in its life and has one third-place finish to show for it. The #7 greyhound, Js Zippinzatscat (the kind of name track announcers must loathe), has finished in the money twice in six starts. He has lifetime winnings of $101.96.

The dogs come bounding out of the gate and chase that silly mechanical rabbit, bumping into each other a bit as they sprint for 550 yards. The whole thing takes a little more than 30 seconds. My dogs are nowhere near the head of the pack.

Once all the dogs cross the finish line, they jump all over each other as they try to get to that mechanical rabbit, which has slipped under a fence. I'm sure greyhounds are smart animals in their own way, but at some point you'd think one of 'em would figure out a couple of things:

1. That rabbit ain't real.
2. The rabbit always slips away just before they can get to it.

It's like they're in a cartoon that always ends the same way.

As I wander around the grandstand area, the track announcer plugs an upcoming special: "We've got a Good Friday fish fry for the better part of the day. Beer batter, baked, or original recipe cod, only $5. Four-piece fried chicken dinner, only $6. . . . This Friday we've got the all-you-can-eat fish fry for $7, that includes mashed potatoes, applesauce, and free admission!"

Sweet.

In addition to the dog races taking place here, you can bet on a few other dog tracks across the country. Some of these races are displayed on monitors scattered throughout the grandstand. I walk past a guy about my age who is focused on a race in Wheeling Downs, in

---

* Boxing an exacta in effect gives you a quinella, but the exacta and quinella pools are separate, so if you've got a quinella on two dogs and I've got an exacta box on the same two dogs, our payouts may not be the same.

West Virginia. As the dogs hit the finish line, the guy says, "Cock-sucker, cocksucker, cocksucker!" I don't think he won.

Over the next few races, I increase the bets to $100 to win, $40 quinellas, and $36 trifecta boxes. I bet on dogs with names such as Iwa Scrappy T and T's Ozzmosis and Who Didit Darcy and Girlgot-rhythm—dogs that don't even come close to winning.

I'm trying to pick medium shots and long shots, but there's a problem: every time I put $100 or more on a dog, it substantially affects the odds. Because I am an idiot, it takes me a while to figure this out. I look around the grandstand, which has a total crowd of what, maybe 300 people? (In 2008, Dairyland had a total attendance of 233,217 for 306 racing dates. That's an average of 762 people per date.) How many of these bettors are risking just a couple of dollars per race? In some cases, the amount I'm wagering on these dogs is more than their entire career winnings. It's a substantial percentage of the entire pool on each race. I put $200 on a dog called Ahk My Life, a 9-1 shot—and almost immediately his odds go down to 7-2. If I bet the favorites, they become even bigger favorites. If I bet a long shot, he's not so much of a long shot any more.

In the ninth race, I put $250 on a dog called A Willin Cowgirl, who is 4-1 in the morning line. She's now 1-9. I'm literally creating a favorite, thus giving some of these folks, who might actually know what they're doing, some fantastically favorable odds.

"Here comes Barney!" the announcer says. Apparently Barney is the name of the mechanical rabbit.

A Willin Cowgirl, who goes off as the 6-5 favorite, has inside posi-tion and runs a solid race, but finishes third, behind Chandelier, who was 5-1 in the morning line but went off at 10-1, thanks in no small part to my bets. In second is Killer Irene, a 5-1 shot.

If you look at the charts from that race, you can see my personal influence on the payouts. Chandelier paid $22.20 to win but just $3.80 to place and $2.80 show, reflecting that there was decent action on the dog to come in second or third, but relatively little activity for it to win. Killer Irene paid $5.40 to place and $4.40 to show. Had my dog,

A Willin Cowgirl, finished first, the payout would have been $4.40 for a win bet. (At 6-5, you'd get $1.20 for every dollar you bet. For a $2 bet, you get back your two bucks plus $1.20 multiplied by 2. Payouts are always listed for $2 bets.)

I've always been an all-or-nothing kind of bettor at the track. I didn't have A Willin Cowgirl "across the board," i.e., separate bets on the dog to win, place, and show. So even though A Willin Cowgirl was a 6-5 favorite to *win*, she paid $5.40 to show. Anyone betting on that dog to come in third was getting better odds than I was for her to come in first. Even in the mad world of gambling, that's some craaaaazy shit.

Yet I still make one more bet on a 9-1 shot that falls to 6-5. The dog comes in second, in a photo finish, paying $13.40 to place and $9.40 to show. Again, more money for coming in second than I would have received had it won.

I exit Greyhound Park, having cashed not a single ticket. For the remainder of the races, the odds return to a normal pattern. The Great Influencer has left the building.

Note from the greyhound track. I didn't realize until later that I had scribbled, "I truly suck at picking these fucking dogs."

Day 15

**Bankroll:
+$1,030**

"At that point I ought to have gone away, but a strange sensation
rose up in me, a sort of defiance of fate, a desire to challenge it,
to put out my tongue at it. I laid down the largest stake allowed—
four thousand gulden—and lost it. Then, getting hot, I pulled out
all I had left, staked it on the same number, and lost again, after
which I walked away from the table as though I were stunned.
I could not even grasp what had happened to me."
—Fyodor Dostoevsky, *The Gambler*

Sometimes I go weeks without sitting on my living room sofa, and
I've always thought of that as a good thing because it's too easy to
lapse into a couch-potato lifestyle when you're a Permanent Bachelor.
Most of my waking work time is spent at the laptop or the desktop,
or in the screening room or on the phone or doing research. At night,
more screenings, family things, social life, poker, poker, poker.

Once in a while, though, even when one is in the middle of a 30-
day gambling binge, there is nothing more relaxing than just plop-

ping down on that couch, remote in hand, cell phone and laptop out of reach. I can click around and just get lost in a 25-minute stretch of a movie I've already seen, or a documentary about what it will be like on Earth when humankind has left the planet, or a virtually meaningless early-season game between the Red Sox and the Yankees, who by law must be on ESPN or Fox every time they play one another.

My friend Julie and I are on the sofa, half-empty crates of P.F. Chang's on the coffee table, and I'm flipping through the channels—because of course the guy controls the remote 97 percent of the time—trying not to think about the gambling I still have to do later on. I'm in a little bit of a funk right now, a little bit "gambled out." That never happens when you're winning, but when you hit a cold streak, the gambling takes so much more out of you, physically and otherwise.

It's not just that I've had a net loss of more than six grand over the last week, though that's sickening enough. Although I'm risking at least $1,000 a day, I'm actually wagering much, much more than that. Consider a session at the blackjack table where you play 60 hands in an hour. If I'm betting $100 per hand, I've just wagered $6,000 in that session. And that's a very conservative estimate. If I'm playing multiple hands online, it might be 200 hands an hour. That's $20,000 in total bets! Of course, I'm not going to lose every hand or win every hand, but still, it's a grind on the psyche to put $100 or more out there on a race, a blackjack hand, a friggin' flip of the coin, whatever, time after time after time after time. By the time I reach the 30-day finish line, I'll have wagered hundreds of thousands of dollars.

Not thinking about that at the moment. Right now I'm watching *30 Days of Night*, a gruesome but stylish zombie/vampire flick starring Josh Hartnett as the good guy and the great and underrated Danny Huston as the lead zombie/vampire guy, who has grotesque fangs and fingernails and talks in an ancient, animalistic tongue. But, hey, he offsets that with some trendy wardrobe choices that make him look like the baddest guy in the nightclub. I didn't much care for *30 Days of Night* when it was released—I thought there was too much gratuitous violence, including a cringe-inducing scene involving a little girl who has been turned into one of the bloodthirsty creatures—but now I'm appreciating the cool cinematography and the energetic performances. Hartnett is really selling this thing, as if he's in a first-rate thriller and not a horror flick with gallons of fake blood spurting everywhere.

But after yet another beheading—*thwack, thwack, thwack* goes Hartnett's ax—Julie grabs the remote, looks at me like I'm a child, and changes the channel, and now we're smack dab in the middle of *21*.

A gambling movie.

Totally different genre, but like *30 Days of Night*, this movie is more about the attractive cast and the cutting-edge camerawork than the story.

"What is this?" says Julie, as Jim Sturgess and Kate Bosworth clutch each other in a Vegas strip club.

I tell her *21* is an adaptation of Ben Mezrich's terrifically entertaining and hugely popular book *Bringing Down the House*, which told the (mostly) true story of a group of MIT whizzes who developed a card-counting system and won hundreds of thousands of dollars in Vegas. (They couldn't call the movie *Bringing Down the House* because that was already the title of a dreadfully unfunny movie from 2003 starring Steve Martin and Queen Latifah.) The filmmakers took a ton of liberties with the book's story (which wasn't 100 percent factual in the first place), glossing up the glamour quotient, neglecting to address any moral issues about avarice, and toning down the material for a PG-13 rating. There's something about Sturgess that screams *vapid*, making him the wrong guy to play a math savant who gets in his over his head and turns into something of a jerkoff. He just struts around as if he's searching for a mirror, reciting his lines with robotic efficiency. The best performances come from Kevin Spacey as the coldly manipulative professor who gets the students together, and Laurence Fishburne as the old-school "loss prevention specialist" who treats card-counters the way a chef would treat a pack of rats in his kitchen. (Remember: card counting isn't illegal, but the casinos

will throw your ass out if they even suspect you're doing it. You're a guest in their house, and their house is designed to separate you from your money. Not only will they stack the odds against you, they won't even let you master a skill that will give you an edge at the table.)

Soon after Sturgess has his moment of makeout with Bosworth, he's in deep shit. Fishburne has him alone in one of those dark and scary Vegas back rooms that still might exist, even though giant corporations run today's big casinos, and the mob is largely a thing of the increasingly distant past. Fishburne roughs up the boy pretty good, and my friend Julie, who does not know the world of gambling except through the stories I tell her, punches my arm.

"This is bad," she says, and I don't think she's talking about the quality of the movie. "It's a bad habit."

What's a good habit? Exercising? Eating the right foods? Doing good deeds like you're a character in *Pay it Forward*? (To stick with the Kevin Spacey motif.) Those aren't habits—those are things you do because you want to stay alive or you want to be a decent human being.

Habits are inherently bad. Smoking, drinking, swearing, partying, gambling. And let me just state for the record: I do not smoke.

Julie asks if I know how to count cards. I tell her I have a basic grasp of it, but I'm nowhere near being good enough to try it in a casino, and I wouldn't try it anyway because I don't want my name in some Black Book, banned for life. I also tell her I do not travel in circles in which anyone faces physical danger over a gambling dispute.

I don't tell her I *have* traveled in such circles. I don't tell her that when I was 22, I was at a poker table where a guy was so deep in debt for the night, he put his car keys into the middle of the pot. I don't tell her I once played in a craps game in the back of a business on the South Side where a guy won three or four grand—and then was held up in the alley as he walked to his car, and we were all pretty sure the guys in the ski masks with the guns were players who had lost big earlier that night, or at least associates of those guys. I don't tell her that I was watching the evening news one night years ago, and the sheriff's police were leading a guy out of his house while the anchor said the suspect had been busted for running a bookmaking operation and for dealing drugs—and I realized I'd been at that guy's house playing a card game called "pimp guts" for stakes well beyond my means just a few weeks earlier.

I'll tell her those stories another time, or maybe never. For now, I tell her I'd love to watch the rest of the movie with her but I've got to get back to work, which of course means I've got to get back to the business of gambling.

The sports room/bar in my house, like the sports rooms/bars in 10 million other American homes, is decorated with memorabilia. I've got framed posters of sports movies such as *Seabiscuit*, *Bull Durham*, and *The Natural*; a framed note from (name-drop alert!) Sylvester Stallone, thanking me after I ranked *Rocky* as my favorite sports movie of all time; a blow-up of the *Sports Illustrated* cover of Scott Podsednik hitting the winning home run for the White Sox in game 2 of the World Series; a collage of poker items; and signed baseballs from boyhood idols of mine such as Luis Aparicio and Dick Allen. (I can't imagine actually asking a young pro athlete for an autograph, but it doesn't seem as childish if the item is from someone you watched as a kid. Even so, most of these pieces were gifts or souvenirs from charity events. As much as I love sports, I'm not that guy who wears a Toews jersey to a Blackhawks game or a Quentin jersey to a Sox game. Millions of fans do it, though, and I'm not putting them down. It's just not my thing.)

In the hallway leading to my rooftop deck, there's a framed, over-sized photo of my favorite horse of all time, captured in his most glorious moment on the track.

The horse is named Birdstone. In 2004, he pulled off one of the bigger upsets in Triple Crown history—and I was backing him all the way.

In May 2004, Smarty Jones won the Kentucky Derby, becoming the first unbeaten horse to win the Derby since Seattle Slew in 1977. *Sports Illustrated* put Smarty Jones on the cover—but there was no SI cover jinx at work here, as Smarty Jones went on to win the Preakness by a record margin.

Smarty Jones was arguably the most popular horse in three decades. Much of the nation was gripped with Triple Crown fever, and a sport that had been looking for a boost for years had great hopes for this undefeated thoroughbred, considered to be the class of the Belmont field by far.

Which meant there was no way I was betting on Smarty Jones.

I've had my periods of hitting the OTB and the Chicago-area tracks on a semiregular basis—maybe once or twice a month—but I've had more years in which I bet on only three races: the Kentucky Derby, the Preakness, and the Belmont. In the 1990s we'd get a group together and go to the Mud Bug in the Old Town neighborhood of Chicago. (The legendary and legendarily cranky and colorful Dave Feldman handicapped horses for the *Chicago Sun-Times* for decades and wrote a book with the horse player's lament as the title: *Woulda, Coulda, Shoulda.* Every time Feldman entered the *Sun-Times* sports department, he expected, and received, applause from the scribes and copyeditors. He was known to hire a musical trio to perform live in the newsroom on a Friday night. When he started experiencing dizzy spells late in his career, he would chain himself to his desk so he wouldn't fall over. The man was a character and then some. One year when we had a group of about 30 in a back room of the Mud Bug for the Derby, Feldman hired a uniformed bugler to play the "Call to the Post"—followed by a uniformed jockey who brought an actual friggin' horse into the facility. The horse skidded around for a bit before it was determined this wasn't the greatest idea in the world, and the poor beast was led back outside.)

When I bet on the Triple Crown races, I wager fairly substantial amounts and I never take the favorite. What's the point? To risk $500 for a payout of maybe twice that? Sure, in the real world even Bernie Madoff wasn't producing those kinds of results, and he was cheating, but in the wagering world there just isn't enough "gamble" in a bet like that to get me pumped.

For the 2004 Belmont, Smarty Jones was a prohibitive favorite, going off at 2-5. That means you'd have to risk $5 to win $2. No doubt many bettors across the nation were buying $2 tickets on Smarty Jones with no intention of taking the profit of less than a dollar you'd get if he stormed to a victory. They'd keep the ticket as a souvenir of the first Triple Crown winner since Affirmed in 1978.

I'm not going to snow you and say I had a special feeling about Birdstone or that I saw something magical in his charts. Yes, Birdstone had won the Champagne Stakes at Belmont as a two-year-old, so I knew he could handle the distance and this particular track. True, his sire was Grindstone, winner of the Kentucky Derby in 1996. And I was familiar with the stellar records of trainer Nick Zito and jockey Edgar Prado.

But Birdstone had finished a distant eighth to Smarty Jones in the Derby, and he hadn't even run in the Preakness. There was no strong reason to believe he could compete with the growing legend that was Smarty Jones. Let's face it, the most attractive thing about Birdstone was the odds. On the morning of the Belmont, I drove over to the Mud Bug to get an early bet down on the race. (My plan was to host a small viewing party in my apartment that evening.) I talked to one of the managers of the facility, who mentioned that an outfielder with the Cubs had already been there. "He likes Birdstone," said the manager.

Me too. Especially with odds of about 35-1.

By post time, the Mud Bug would be jam-packed, but at this mid-morning juncture there was no waiting to place your bets. Without hesitation, I marched to the window and placed $400 to win on Birdstone. Then I stopped to get a Diet Coke and watch an early race or two—and before I left, I decided I'd put another two hondo on Bird-stone. Losing another $200 wouldn't mean anything, but losing the opportunity to win several thousand more would have bugged me. (This is the thought process of many a big winner: *I should have bet even more. Why didn't I bet even more?*)

That evening I had about a half dozen friends over to watch the race. A record crowd of more than 120,000 had turned out at Bel-mont Park, and millions more were watching on TV. As you might expect, the prerace coverage was all about Smarty Jones and how this courageous thoroughbred had captured America's heart. Handicap-pers across the nation were nearly unanimously behind Smarty Jones. There was some talk about Rock Hard Ten or Purge springing the upset—but nobody was seriously suggesting that would happen.

The crowd roared when the gates opened.

"They're off in the 136th Belmont," said the track announcer. "Smarty Jones off to a good beginning today. . . ."

Not a mention of Birdstone until the horses were past the club-house turn. He was in sixth, seemingly a nonfactor.

Past the half-mile mark, the announcer bellowed, "And Smarty Jones has taken the lead, as they begin their long journey down the Belmont back stretch . . . and Smarty Jones has to hold onto that lead for just one minute more. . . . Birdstone commences a rally, he's six lengths from the front . . ."

I looked over at a buddy who knew I had more than a few dollars on Birdstone. He arched his eyebrows as if to say, "You gotta be kid-ding me."

The announcer continued his call:

"Around the turn, and it's Smarty Jones, he lets it out a notch, to lead by a length and a half. . . . They're coming to the top of the stretch, Smarty Jones has a four-length lead . . . and Smarty Jones enters the stretch to the roar of 120,000, but Birdstone is going to make him earn it today . . . it's been 26 years [since the last Triple Crown], it's just one furlong away . . . they're coming down to the finish, can Smarty Jones hold on? Here comes Birdstone! Birdstone surges past, Birdstone wins the Belmont Stakes. Smarty Jones was valiant but vanquished but finishing second . . . and so this Triple Crown remains vacated . . . and this magical Triple Crown trail of Smarty Jones comes to an end. . . ."

The NBC cameras focused on Smarty Jones' owners, heartbroken in the stands. The announcers talked about the disappointment of Smarty Jones losing. The first interview on the track was with Smarty Jones's jockey. It was as if Birdstone was a villain, and who wants to talk about the villain? The race was over for a full three minutes before they got around to focusing on Birdstone and jockey Edgar Prado—and even Prado expressed his sympathy for the Smarty Jones team.

Meanwhile, the Belmont crowd was in stunned near-silence. Not so much at the casa, where my buddy had started cackling wildly during the amazing stretch run, when Birdstone seemed to be hopelessly behind before catching and passing Smarty Jones with such a ferocious charge that there was no doubt about the result.

As I recall, my first reaction was something along the lines of "Holy shit!"

After some high-fiving and hugging, we saw the results posted on TV. Birdstone had gone off as a 36-1 long shot at Belmont, and I'd probably have the same odds for my OTB tickets. That's $74 for each $2 wager, and I had $600 on the nose—meaning a profit of about $22,000, give or a take a few hundred.

We wound up celebrating at a restaurant called Bijan's with more than a few bottles of Dom Pérignon. On Monday morning, I drove to the Mud Bug and claimed my winnings—the largest amount I'd ever won on any single bet in my life.

A few weeks later, a friend gifted me with the awesome framed photo depicting the moment when Birdstone shot by Smarty Jones in the stretch. The race isn't technically over in this photo, but it's all over.

Edgar Prado had signed the photo. I hung it in my sports bar, a constant reminder of the greatest single moment in my wagering career.

Birdstone was a horse I'd never forget.

Five years later I'm at the Stretch Run, the beautifully appointed OTB, bar, and restaurant that sits on a corner of LaSalle Street, so close to my place I can see it from the balcony. It's late afternoon/early evening, and there's a decent-sized crowd spread about the place. Some couples, guys in groups of two or three, a number of solo horseplayers. There's a small monitor at my table, a betting machine about three feet away, and multiple monitors above the bar showing races at Pocono, Penn National, Windsor, Charles Town, Northville, and other tracks.

In the old days when you went to the track, you'd have to wait 20 minutes or so between races. More than enough time to study the racing form and make your picks. Now, every time one race ends, I scan the monitors and find another race that's just minutes away. Often I'll have two races going at once.

The jukebox is playing "Money" by Pink Floyd. Too obvious, I know, but that's what it's playing. Outside, it's still bright. On my short walk over through this neighborhood of condos and restaurants, bars and hotels, a few upscale little shops, I passed families and couples and businesspeople, all going about the end of their day in normal fashion. Traffic on Ontario was particularly thick, as commuters made their way to the on-ramp leading to the Dan Ryan and Kennedy and Eisenhower Expressways.

Part of me feels like I'm getting away with something. *All those poor regular stiffs going about their business, and look what you're doing!* Another part of me feels like a degenerate. *All those normal people with their gamble-free lives, and look what you're doing!* They're not sitting here getting a knot in the stomach because of a $200 bet on the #11 horse to win the fourth race at Penn National.

I drop $20 on an exacta bet at Northville, $75 on the #1 horse in the 3rd at Charles Town, another $120 on the 14th at Dover, hundreds and hundreds more on races at Pompano, Pocano, even Balmoral—and who the hell even invented harness racing anyway? I mean, you want to talk about a ridiculous spectacle.

Occasionally I hit a winner. A little more than $400 profit on one race, another $210 a half hour later. But the losses are piling up with much greater frequency.

I bet on horses based on their career earnings. I make choices based on the handicapper's selection. Sometimes I go with a horse because it has dropped in class and is facing easier competition. Sometimes I go with a hunch, or a name that has a personal meaning. (Gander at the lineup for nearly any race at any time and you should be able to find at least one horse with a name that has some kind of a personal connection. It's like reading your horoscope. You can always find something relatable.) Sometimes I just bet.

There's a horse named Alexaastrodinaire. I know a girl named Alex. Good enough!

Drink Up. I just drank up.

Artistic Fool. I'm one of those things.

Mocha Latte. I like mocha lattes.

B Murray. Love the Bill Murray.

Let's Talk About Me. Um . . .

And so it goes. That's not the name of a horse, that's what I'm saying: and so it goes. I rack up loss after loss after loss. Outside, the sun has departed and the lights are on in the city, and the daytime bustle has given way to the nighttime buzz. I'm getting cross-eyed from reading the program. I already switched from beer to coffee, and now I'm downing Diet Cokes. I'm not sure exactly how much I'm down, but the wad of loser tickets in my left pocket is thicker than the wad of cash in my right pocket.

As I look over the selections for the sixth at Charles Town, an ad at the bottom of the program says: "Call 1-800-GAMBLER (426-2537) for confidential help with problem gambling." Yeah, I suppose some people need that. In the meantime, I'm trying to make one big bet to cover all the losses of the past few hours. I put $300 to win on the #5

horse, Laura's Chance, at 12-1, and I take a $40 exacta box, pairing Laura's Chance with a medium shot called Sweet Whispers. If Laura's Chance wins, I'll be up plenty for the day. If Laura's Chance and Sweet Whispers finish 1 and 2 in either order, I'll be a big-ass winner for the week.

Long before the home stretch, my chances are slim and none, and slim just left town. *Fuck, fuck, fuck, fuckity fuck.*

Day 16

Bankroll:
−$870

Wwe are down but we are not out. We are down but we are not down. We are down but we have *faith*.

This is the thing about the bet. Winning, of course, is better than losing—but making the bet might be even more exhilarating than the moment of triumph.

If you've ever been on a flight to Vegas on a Thursday afternoon or a Friday morning, you know what I'm talking about—especially if you're on one of those open-seating flights with no first class or business section, where the crowd tends to be a bit younger and you see groups of 6, 10, 12 boarding the plane, all wearing T-shirts that identify them as members of the Bachelor Party or the 25th Birthday Party or some other getaway weekend blowout. Sometimes the collective mood on these flights is downright giddy. Guys will be playing cards to get in the mood to gamble. Couples will be nuzzling and cooing as they talk about the weekend plans. The cocktails will be

flowing. You could put that same collection of people on a flight to Paris or Rome or some other dream destination, and they wouldn't be that excited.

It's the same way at a craps table that is starting to heat up (though of course we don't believe in streaks, at least not from an intellectual standpoint), or a blackjack table where a collection of strangers have bonded over their mutual "hatred" of the dealer, or at a major poker tournament when the announcer says "Shuffle up and deal!" and everyone has the same chip count and the same dream—winning the whole thing. I've seen guys sit down at World Series of Poker events, nearly bursting with enthusiasm as they stack their chips, shake everyone's hand, and gush, "Good luck, fellas!" And if you want to see true group behavior madness, check out the high-stakes baccarat tables, where the players act as if all their good luck rituals and hearty cheers actually have bearing on a game that has no more inherent strategy than a flip of the coin.

We believe. No matter what has happened in the past, when we sit down at a table or we drive to the track or we log on to our favorite gambling site, we believe today is the day we are going to strike it big. If I'm entered in the massive Sunday Million tournament on Poker-Stars, with 5,000 or 6,000 entrants, I don't look at the overwhelming international field and calculate that my chances of winning are only a little better than my chances of flapping my arms and levitating—I look at that first prize of $225,000 and think, *That could be mine.*

That is how I felt when I played the $5 craps games on the Iowa riverboats in the early 1990s, and that's how I felt when I hit the $100 blackjack tables in Vegas at the start of the new millennium, and that's how I feel today as I drive to a nearby riverboat casino for a round of blackjack, craps, and roulette.

Today is going to be different than yesterday. I don't even remember yesterday. Today the cards, the dice, and that spinning white ball are all going to tumble in my favor.

Day 17

**Bankroll:
–$3,470**

BOOKIE: "Listen, I'm gonna tell you something I never told a customer before. Personally, I never made a bet in my life. You know why? Because I've observed firsthand what with seeing the different kinds of people that are addicted to gambling— what we would call degenerates. I've noticed there's one thing that makes all of them the same. You know what that is?"
AXEL: "Yes. They're all looking to lose."
BOOKIE: "You mean you know that!"

— *The Gambler* (1974)

They're calling him the alleged Craigslist Killer.

Philip Markoff, 23, a second-year medical student, is charged with robbery, kidnapping, and murder in the shooting death of a 26-year-old massage therapist who had advertised on Craiglist, the immensely popular Internet classified ad site. Markoff was also charged with robbing a Las Vegas prostitute in a Boston hotel room a few days prior to the killing of the massage therapist.

The Craigslist hook dominates the headlines—but I'm wondering if Markoff might actually be an alleged Blackjack Killer.

From a Boston TV station's Web site:

Accused Craigslist killer repeatedly visited casino
Investigators looking at gambling motive in crimes

Markoff and his fiancée, Megan McAllister, were headed to Foxwoods Casino in Connecticut when he was arrested.

"As we explore various motives for the robberies, gambling is certainly a motive we will look at," says the district attorney pursuing the case.

Two days after the robbery of the prostitute, Markoff was at Foxwoods. Two days after the murder of the massage therapist, he was at Foxwoods again.

As of this writing, we don't know if Markoff is guilty or if a gambling habit motivated him to attack and rob these poor women. After Markoff's arrest, his fiancée rushed to his defense, e-mailing the media:

Unfortunately you were given the wrong information as was the public. Philip is a beautiful person inside out and could not hurt a fly! A police officer in Boston [or many] is trying to make big bucks by selling this false story to the TV stations. What else is new?? Philip is an intelligent man who is just trying to live his life so if you could leave us alone we would greatly appreciate it. We expect to marry in August and share a wonderful life together.

For a while the fiancée even kept their wedding Web site running, complete with gift registry. But as the evidence mounted, the shell-shocked woman grew silent and the wedding Web site was taken down.

Despite all the energy and optimism I had going into yesterday's action, my blackjack/roulette/craps outing started with a whimper and ended with a whine. From the moment I entered the casino armed with $2,500 in crisp $100 bills, through the trips to the ATM for more cash, to the moment I walked back to the car reeking of smoke and with my tail between my legs (for some odd reason craving a Big Mac, and I eat a Big Mac about once a year), nothing went right. There was never a single moment when I was ahead. I just took a pounding. If every gambling day was like that, I would have stopped 20 years ago.

Dammit.

At least today's adventure is a charity event, bringing with it a giant glass of cool perspective.

Shortly after the poker boom in the early years of the new millennium, organizations all over the country started organizing hold 'em tournaments to go along with the long-established "casino nights." From state to state the rules vary, but it usually works like this: you can hold a charity poker tournament as long as you're established as a legitimate organization and the prizes come in a form other than cold hard cash. Often the first prize is a seat at the Main Event of the World Series of Poker, worth some $10,000; in lieu of that, it might be a Visa gift card worth $3,000 or $5,000. They'll also award weekend trips, flat-screen TVs, gift baskets, dinner certificates, and other prizes donated by various sponsors.

I've played in about 50 of these tournaments—mostly in the Chicago area, but also in Los Angeles and Las Vegas. (See the sidebar in this chapter.) Sometimes I play to win. Doesn't mean I will win, but I give it the same effort I would if I were at a World Series of Poker bracelet event and I were shooting for a six-figure first prize. On other occasions, I'm the host or one of the designated "celebrity bounties" for the tournament, and it's just as important for me to roam around, to grab the microphone for some snappy banter, or to get into some crazy hands with the opponents at my table who have paid a cash entry fee for the chance to play poker

with a genuine celebrity like a football player or a hip-hop star, and instead wound up with what's-his-name, the guy from the movie show.

A while back I was playing in a benefit tourney for the March of Dimes. This was just before the recession hit, and fields for these events would routinely number in the three hundreds or more. There were probably four hundred entrants in this tournament, held in a massive banquet room in downtown Chicago. The buy-in was $350. They were going to raise a lot of money that evening, which is the real and only purpose that matters—though not everyone sees it that way. (More on that in a moment.)

As so often happens at these events, there was a guy at my table who had never played in any kind of a poker tournament in his life and had only a very fundamental understanding of the game. I believe he was on one of the organizing committees for the event. He cheerfully admitted his lack of experience to all of us as we made our introductions and settled into our seats.

On the very first hand, I was dealt pocket Aces, and I made a big raise. Of course, nobody folds any more, whether you're playing in a tough cash game or a loose charity event, so I got three callers, including the rookie.

The flop came Q-5-K.

I made a big bet. It's a charity tournament. What the heck. Unless someone has K-Q or has flopped a set, I should be good.

Everyone folded except the rook, who pushed all his chips into the middle and said, "I raise—I bet everything," which in a charity tournament is the same as declaring one is all-in.

With only about 30 percent of my starting stack left, I called and turned over my Aces.

He turned over Q-5 off-suit. Of course he called my original bet of four or five times the big blind; he had a Queen and another card!

The turn and the river were blanks for me, and just like that, I was out of the tournament and the rookie was the chip leader. I shook hands with everyone and congratulated the guy, who asked if I'd stick around and help him out. I said I'd be glad to sit in, just as soon as I grabbed a drink.

Walking around the bustling room, I ran into the tournament director, who was from the Majestic Star casino in Gary, Indiana.

"You having trouble finding your seat?" he said, assuming I was just arriving.

"No," I replied. "I got knocked out."

He laughed.

"I'm serious. Pocket Aces, cracked on the first hand."

He grabbed a microphone, took to the stage, and announced to everyone that yours truly was out of the tournament, the first player to be eliminated. Applause!

A few minutes later, they declared that in the interest of raising more money for the cause, the first hundred players knocked out would have the option of buying back into the tournament. I bought back in and told the guy who had knocked me out he'd have to scrape by on his own—and maybe that wouldn't be a problem, seeing as how he had separated me from my chips on the very first hand of the night.

Here's the thing though: even if you suffer a horrible beat on the very first hand, you shrug it off and remember the reason you're there. It's not hard to do that; all you have to do is read the brochure or chat with one of the families that have been hit hard by whatever affliction or problem is being addressed on this particular night. When a 10-year-old girl gives a speech about the seven operations she's had and the friends she's made in the hospital, when some young parents tell you only the surface details of the unimaginable ordeal they've been through, when a doctor or a nurse tells you some sobering statistic about the cost of treating one patient with a particular illness—after that you're going to lament your bad luck at the fucking card table? Really?

Believe it or not, I've seen it happen. Although the great majority of players at these tournaments have the right attitude and the proper perspective, I've seen guys pound the table and curse after losing,

berate the dealers for bad beats, complain to the tournament direc-
tors about the blind structures, or bitch about the prizes for making
the final table.

On this 17th day of my adventure, the tournament is a benefit for
the Cystic Fibrosis Foundation. We're in a large room at the Marriott
Downtown Chicago Magnificent Mile Hotel, where they're serving
drinks and "heavy hors d'oeuvres," and a pianist is filling the room with
pop tunes as more than 700 guests play blackjack, craps, and roulette.

The entry fee to the hold 'em tournament is $500. We've got about
250 players. First prize is a seat to the Main Event of the World Series
of Poker in the summer of 2009.

Four or five of my poker buddies are also playing in this tournament. None of us expect to win the thing, but we're gonna try tonight.
We're also going to make sure we have a good time and we spend
some time hanging out—so even if there's not an official break, we
take turns visiting one another's tables or we meet at the bar.

The atmosphere tonight is light and friendly. My table features a
couple of tough players I recognize from the boats in northwest Indiana, and about a half-dozen seriously amateur amateurs. A pleasant
woman sitting to my right has one of those laminated cards ranking the top hold 'em hands. I help her with the mechanics of posting
blinds, announcing raises, folding one's hand.

From a few tables over, my friend Tim sends me a text:

"This guy next to me is being a real jerk."

I stand up and see a guy who's probably in his late 20s, sporting
the obligatory two-day beard, baseball cap, headphones, sunglasses.
His shirt identifies him as a representative of one of the major online
poker sites, but I'm not going to say which one because anyone should
be embarrassed to be associated with this fucker based on the behavior I'm about to witness.

Maybe a half hour later, I've got a healthy chip stack going, so I
wander over to see how Tim is doing. He rolls his eyes, indicating
Mr. Jerk, who is in the process of helping the dealer figure out the
division of a pot in which two players are all-in and a third has them

covered. If Mr. Jerk did this in a regulation tournament, he might get his hands slapped, but some of the dealers at tonight's event are volunteers who don't do this for a living, and often they'll be grateful for some intervention to move things along, even from a know-it-all asshole.

A couple of hands later, Mr. Jerko gets into a big pot with a young woman who is wearing a lovely cocktail dress and seems more than a little intimidated by the action at the table. Like the woman at my table, she has one of those laminated hand-ranking cards next to her drink, indicating she has rarely if ever played live hold 'em.

She's not sure what to do. She wants to show her hand to somebody, but evidently Mr. Jerko has complained already about such "collusion." (Guys like him have no problem breaking the rules by touching the chips, but God forbid somebody else violate the sanctity of the game in a manner that might hurt this hand.)

Mr. Jerko pounds his hand on the table and notes that the blinds are about to go up. And then he says it:

"Clock!"

Tim looks at me. Did this guy really just call for a clock?

For those unfamiliar with tournament play: If you're in a hand and you feel your opponent is stalling for an unreasonable amount of time, you can call for a clock. A supervisor will come over, and if he determines that a sufficient amount of time has indeed passed, he will inform the indecisive and/or grandstanding player she has one minute to make a decision. If the stalling player doesn't do anything at that point, her hand will automatically be folded. (According to the rules, you don't have to be active in the hand to call a clock. Anyone at the table can do so. Usually it's considered bad form to call a clock if you're not involved in a hand. A young pro named Tiffany Michelle came under heavy fire on the poker forums when she called a clock in the Main Event during a hand in which she was not involved. Michelle said TV didn't accurately reflect what happened—that at least 15 minutes had passed before she called for a clock.)

In all the tournaments I've ever played in, I've been at maybe three tables where someone called for a clock. In each case, we were playing for a lot of money, it was deep into the tournament, and the guy who called for the clock had a legitimate reason for asking management to intervene so we could get on with it.

But in a charity tournament? When you're involved in a hand with someone who is obviously confused and nervous, not stalling or messing with you?

"Did that guy just call for a clock?" I say it plenty loud enough for him to hear me. Because I couldn't quite believe it.

"Clock!" the guy says again, louder than the first time.

Another player at the table says, "Come on, man. You're going to call a clock on her? Take it easy."

"Hey, I'm playing for a $10,000 seat," replies Mr. Jerko.

"Right," I say. "It's not like we're at a *charity event* or anything."

First of all: there are still at least two hundred players left in the tournament. It's not as if you're at the final table, with just three other contenders for that Main Event seat. And even if that were the case, it's still a charity event! You want to seriously play for a $10,000 seat, then go enter a cash game satellite or an online tournament, not a benefit for the Cystic Fibrosis Foundation, in which the prizes are utterly secondary to the spirit of the evening and the money they're trying to raise.

What a colossal asshole.

At this point I have to walk away, because I feel as if I'm about five seconds from laying into this guy, and that's not the right way to act at a benefit either.

I'm told later that the woman folded her hand before anyone could put her on the clock. About an hour after the incident, I show up just as Tim is in a showdown with Mr. Jerko. On the turn, Mr. Jerko is about drawing dead to a 4 for the inside straight. Of course he screams *Four!* as if he's Mike Matusow facing elimination in heads-up play at a championship event—but his demands are not met, and he is out of the tournament, just a hundred places or so short of that $10,000 seat he was "playing for."

That's a shame.

Playing loose and aggressive, I make it deep into the tournament. At one point I defend my big blind with 9-4 of diamonds and I flop a flush, eventually knocking out the guy who had raised me with pocket Kings. When he sees my cards—a worse hand than the Q-5 that knocked me out of that tournament a few years ago—he shakes his head at my idiotic call, but he also shakes my hand and says, "I had a great time. Good luck, everyone." And then his wife takes a picture of us as I apologize for the 9-4 of diamonds.

"No problem," he says. Turns out he's one the organizers of tonight's event. If he won, he was just going to donate his prize back to the cause anyway.

You meet so many people like that at these events. Professionals who have dedicated their careers to doing good things. Volunteers who give up evenings and weekends to work for a good cause. Health care workers. Brave kids fighting diseases and smiling through it. Families who should be cursing the heavens but instead are thanking God for the progress being made against some deadly disease. They outnumber the Mr. Jerko's of the world by 100-1.

And this is why I do not particularly care when I'm eliminated with about 40 players left. I had pretty much considered this a day off from the "real" gambling anyway. The entry fee was more like a donation. In a way I should be grateful for Mr. Jerko and his dreadful behavior. It's given me a healthy shot of perspective just when I need it the most. There are a lot of people in this building tonight who wish the worst problem of the month was losing several thousand dollars on cards and horses.

Playing in a Celebrity Tourney

Virtually every time he grabs the microphone, Charles Barkley tells Casey Affleck he wishes Brad Pitt had shot and killed him in that movie the two actors did together.

"I hated you in that movie," Barkley tells Affleck. "I wanted them to kill you. I wish Brad Pitt would have shot you."

The movie was titled *The Assassination of Jesse James by the Coward Robert Ford*. Affleck played Robert Ford. Pitt played Jesse James. The title might have been a hint Pitt wasn't going to shoot Affleck at any point.

We're at the Rio in Las Vegas for the second annual Ante Up for Africa poker tournament, which runs just before the start of the Main Event of the World Series of Poker. Hosted by Don Cheadle and poker pro Annie Duke, the event raises funds for charities that provide assistance to the survivors of the ethnic cleansing in Darfur.

Here's the deal: Poker pros, poker-playing celebrities, and amateur players with deep pockets each pay a $5,000 entry fee. Because the event is officially tied to the World Series of Poker, the entry fees do not go to the charity. There's a prize pool, and all participants agree to donate at least half their winnings to the charity.

Last year, most of the players who finished in the money—including the top two—donated *all* their winnings.

A word here about the whole donate-the-winnings thing.

It's always a feel-good moment when somebody wins the Jumbo Grand Prize at a charity raffle—and then gives the prize right back to the worthy cause.

The host grabs the mike and says something like, "Now the moment we've all been waiting for: the winner of our Jumbo Grand Prize, a package worth more than $25,000, is . . . That Really Rich Guy!"

Then That Really Rich Guy takes the microphone and says, "Ladies and gentlemen, I've been blessed with such good fortune in my life—so I'm donating my winnings right back!"

The crowd goes nuts, That Really Rich Guy gets a standing ovation, and the woman who spent a year begging businesses to donate to the Jumbo Grand Prize package smiles gamely while thinking, "Why, you spotlight-stealing bastard."

Even if you're blessed with good fortune, winning a prize is winning a prize. It gives you instant license to do something silly or extravagant, like hosting a party or buying an obscenely expensive piece of jewelry or buying courtside tickets to a Bulls game. So, fine: kudos to anyone who gives back his or her raffle winnings. This practice has become a mini-trend of sorts in recent years, to the point where you almost expect the big winner to give back the raffle prize. But if you don't want to give back the prize, does that make you a heel?

Last year, a friend of mine from Chicago joined me for the first Ante Up for Africa tournament. They gave us forms asking us to pledge at least half of our winnings to the Enough Project and the International Rescue Committee—two of the finest charities in the world. As far as I know, everyone signed—everyone except my buddy, that is. He's against "forced charity," and besides, he had plans of his own for any winnings. He was going to donate to an equally worthy cause of his choosing—the inner-city school he runs on the South Side of Chicago.

I started that tournament sitting between expert poker commentator Phil Gordon and Casey Affleck. Also at the table:

Cheadle, Willie Garson from *Sex and the City*, Cheryl Hines from *Curb Your Enthusiasm*, and Doyle Brunson, the Babe Ruth of poker. It was, as they say, sick. My friend and I survived for quite a while—he came close to making the money—but we were eliminated before the final table.

When it was down to the final two players, one announced he'd be donating not 50 percent but all of his winnings to the charities. The other player followed suit immediately. Between them, they'd be "kicking back" more than $385,000.

The crowd roared. Flash bulbs popped. Celebrities hugged the players. Journalists called it the feel-good moment of the entire tournament.

And I was thinking: If I'd made it to the final two and a guy announced he was donating all his winnings to the charity, I would have been in a quandary. Couldn't I keep half, as per the pretournament agreement, spread it around to family, friends, and worthy causes of my choosing, maybe even keep a little for myself? Maybe I would have wilted under the spotlight—but I know what my friend would have said to Mr. Benevolent: "Good for you, now sit your ass down and let's play poker."

I've played in a number of these charity poker events in recent years, including an outdoor tournament at the Playboy Mansion earlier this summer. (Sorry, I was going to ask *you* to come along, but I thought you were busy that weekend.) But the second annual Ante Up for Africa tournament is by far the most star-studded. A partial roster of the celebrity participants: Ben and Casey Affleck, Jason Alexander, Charles Barkley, Don Cheadle,

Matt Damon, Shannon Elizabeth, Ray Romano, Adam Sandler, Jennifer Tilly, and members of Alice in Chains, Anthrax, and Fall Out Boy. This next list will mean something only if you're a poker fan, but participating pros include Andy Bloch, Chris "Jesus" Ferguson, Joe Hachem, Phil Hellmuth, Phil Ivey, Phil "the Unabomber" Laak, Michael Mizrachi, Greg Raymer, Erik Seidel, and many, many more World Series of Poker bracelet winners.

With 2006 World Series of Poker Main Event champion Jamie Gold at a charity tournament at the Playboy Mansion.

For the first hour or so, I sit to the right of the classy Joe Hachem, winner of the 2005 Main Event. ("Aussie, Aussie, Aussie!") I trap the Unabomber with a check-raise. I surrender pocket Jacks against Seidel's monster raise; he'll later tell me he had pocket Kings and I made a great laydown. I go all-in with A-Q against Jason Alexander, who goes into the tank for a good while before calling me with the same hand. (We're happy to chop the pot.) Barkley gives me a hard time about liking the movie *Wanted*. ("That film was

Across the table from poker pro Phil "the Unabomber" Laak.

At a charity tournament in Las Vegas next to some guy named Ben, who seems to know the game pretty well.

turrible," he says, sounding just like a Charles Barkley impersonator.) Romano chats me up during the break about *Hancock*, and Bloch wants to compare notes about *21*, which, as I've mentioned, was based on the true story of the MIT blackjack team, of which Bloch was an original member.

There are so many poker pros and celebrity participants, you're virtually guaranteed table time with a Matt Damon or a Ben Affleck or a famous champion. The event is also open to the public, with fans wearing out the camera button on their cell phones and cheering every dramatic hand.

Phil Hellmuth, who calls himself the world's greatest hold 'em player and is probably right—at least when it comes to tournament play—provides running commentary, with Barkley—a.k.a. the world's worst gambler—often stealing the microphone to offer his unique take on the world. (Ten hours later, Barkley will still be offering me his unique take on the world as we do Lemon

Bantering with Charles Barkley at a tournament in Vegas.

Drops at a lounge in Caesars Palace, but that's a story for another day.) Although the atmosphere is casual, everyone is playing to win.

For the first several rounds, I'm among the chip leaders, because I'm just that good. (Catching straights and flushes also helps.) But then my Q-Q is bested by an A-7, halving my stack. Later, with about 30 tables left, I go all in with Q-Q again, only to lose when Dan Shak's K-Q catches a King on the turn.

I hate pocket Queens. And, no, that's not a joke about short cross-dressers.

The final table includes Romano, Jerry Cantrell of Alice in Chains, Casey Affleck (who swore to me before the tourney that he didn't play much poker), and a number of pros and amateurs. A pro named John "the World" Hennigan winds up winning, and he donates the entire $136,860 first prize to charity. (I want to know how you can get a nickname like "the World." That's a good nickname.)

With the addition of gimmicks like celebrity bounties, bleachers for the fans, maybe some closed-circuit TV, and about a half-dozen other brilliant ideas I'm willing to share for free, this tournament could blow up. In the meantime, it's about as much fun as you can have in Vegas without seeing Celine Dion making a guest appearance in a Cirque du Soleil show.

Day 18

Bankroll:
–$4,470

An envelope arrives in the mail from New Jersey. Inside is a check for $1,000 and a note from Artie Lange:

Richard:

Here's your fucking money. Good luck with your book about gambling. You gave me a great idea for my second book. My second book will be about the dangers of gambling with someone writing a book about gambling.

Alright man, I'm going to let you go. I know you're probably busy reviewing the new Hannah Montana movie. I would feel like such an insider if you could send me the review before it's published. I'm curious to know if it's something I could bring a date to or if it's something I could enjoy with the fellas!

Take care Fruity!

Artie Lange

Funnyman Artie Lange makes good on our $1,000 bet on a college hoops game.

The check clears. Thanks, Artie.

If there's no traffic, it takes only a little more than an hour to drive from Chicago to the Four Winds Casino Resort in New Buffalo, Michigan. After exiting I-94, it's just a couple of blocks to the entrance, after which you take a pleasant, winding, tree-lined road to the casino complex, which looks like a giant Disney World lodge.

The main entrance consists of a large rotunda with two fireplaces, in honor of the casino's owners: the Pokagon Band of Potawatomi Indians, a.k.a. "Keepers of the Fire." Wooden beams, copper, and stone abound, giving the appearance of a rustic getaway—but there's also a fancy new car on display, and you could be the lucky winner!

Four Winds is one of about 425 Indian gaming facilities nation-wide. Since 1988, when the government passed the Indian Gaming Regulatory Act, a.k.a. the We Feel Guilty So Here's Your Chance to Make Big Bucks Act, hundreds of tribes have depended on casinos of all shapes and sizes to survive. There's often controversy about who gets the money and how it is distributed, and in some cases the behind-the-scenes backers (who are not Native Americans) make the lion's share of profits. (It doesn't help that the original legislation was murky and filled with loopholes.)

What's beyond dispute is that a lot of people are getting rich from these casinos. Over the last few years, Indian casinos have raked in an average of more than $25 *billion* in revenue. According to the *Indian*

Gaming Industry Report, Indian gaming facilities support some 340,000 jobs paying some $12 billion in wages.

The Four Winds is the largest employer in the New Buffalo region, supporting some 3,500 jobs in the community—nearly 2,500 at the casino itself. In the spring of 2009, after much delay and dispute, the Pokagon tribe handed over a check for more than $6 million to a board appointed to share funds with local communities, in accordance with an agreement that was struck when the Four Winds project was announced. That $6 million check represented just 2 percent of Four Winds' profits from its electronic gaming machines.

In addition to the 125,000-square-foot gaming floor, with more than 3,000 slots, 100 table games, and a World Poker Tour room with electronic poker tables, Four Winds has a 165-room hotel, a couple of nice restaurants, a Starbucks, a few boutique stores, and a large arcade area so the kids have something to do while Mom and Dad play Wheel of Fortune or try their luck at mini-baccarat.

Armed with a giant iced latte, I hit the gimmick games. Pai gow poker, Let It Ride, Crazy 4.

A word about these types of games: I hate 'em. (OK, that's three words.) They're the gambling equivalent of "Hallmark holidays" such as Sweetest Day or Secretary's Day—manufactured variations on traditional games that don't need to be screwed with in the first place. If you enjoy playing pai gow poker or Blackjack Switch (you're dealt two hands and you can swap cards between hands), cheers to you, but you might as well be playing bingo.

And that goes triple for baccarat. Just because it has roots in the 15th century and it was once the game of choice for James Bond, just because some of the biggest high rollers in the world and some of the biggest celebrities in the world love to play this game, doesn't change the fundamental, indisputable truth: it's a silly, maddeningly simplistic, pure-luck game with no more strategy than old maid or war.

Here's the deal with baccarat. Cards 2 through 9 carry their face value. Face cards and 10s are 0, and Aces are 1. The highest score you can get is a 9. If you have a 7+3, you have a 10, which is the same as a 0.

You can bet on the player or the banker. Or a tie. After that, there are no decisions to be made. You have to draw and stand on certain hands, as does the dealer. There are all kinds of traditions—e.g., the player at the table with the largest bet gets to turn over the cards. Many players engage in elaborate, time-consuming rituals involving good luck charms, spinning around in a circle, rubbing their hands together and chanting, whatever. You can participate in as many of these rituals as you like, and your influence on the outcome is the same as the influence wielded by a face-painting fan rooting for his favorite team in the Super Bowl.

(The difference between baccarat and mini-baccarat is that in the latter, the dealer handles all the cards, meaning the game moves faster.)

Amazingly, some of the richest gamblers in the world would rather play baccarat than poker or blackjack or even craps. That's why you'll see baccarat tables in a separate, roped-off area with elegantly attired dealers and stepped-up security—whales who are playing for $25,000 a hand are entitled to their privacy. These players indulge their superstitions and they keep track of "trends" with scorecards. They will literally rip up losing hands, howl at their losses, and sing when they win. It's all very elaborate and ritualistic, and it's all a bunch of nonsense. They're still just betting on the flip of a coin.

The house edge in baccarat isn't all that bad, actually—but unless you're playing for insane stakes, the game itself is deadly dull. I almost don't care that I'm losing.

And so it goes with the other gimmick games I play, as well as a few forays into roulette and the slots bearing the logos of eBay and other pop culture staples. (You see the *Star Wars* slots and you think: good thing George Lucas figured out a way to make a little spare change.) I've pledged to try as many games as possible for the sake of the book, and I've put in my time with the gimmick games, and I'll probably never play them again in my life. But at least I pick up a nice Four Winds baseball cap at the souvenir shop on my way out.

Day 19

**Bankroll:
-$5,770**

Not all gambling is pressure packed or mercenary in nature. Some of the biggest laughs I ever have are at the poker table, playing with friends for relatively low stakes while we debate everything from the American education system to the music of Bruce Springsteen to the best superhero movies to the economy. At times the action will come to a standstill as somebody demonstrates the latest application on his iPhone, or we get into an extended laughfest about this guy's dating misadventures or that guy's problems with his boss at work. We're eating chicken and sliders and pizza and other kill-me-now food; we're drinking beer or Gatorade or scotch on the rocks; we're watching the Sox on one screen and an episode of *Flight of the Conchords* on another screen.

You still want to win the minitournament or come out ahead in the cash game. It still sucks when you're knocked out or you reach your limit of two rebuys and it's time to hit the sofa or head home. But

that's not what these nights are about. The poker really is secondary. It's not about the cards. It's about the friends.

When everybody in the family puts in a dollar on the Kentucky Derby and the eight-year-old wins the pot, it's hilarious. When you're in an NCAA pool and the office assistant who has never seen a game in her life is far ahead of the know-it-all ex-jocks who stand around the water cooler second-guessing Coach K., fantastic. If you buy a lottery ticket, just one ticket, every week and you sit in front of the TV with your wife, dreaming your dreams of hitting it big, why not? When you're in a big tournament in Vegas and you meet up with your buddies during breaks to share bad-beat stories and discuss strategy, it's a hell of a lot more fun than when you don't really know anyone else in the tourney and you spend the down time texting or calling friends with updates.

Those annual trips to Vegas, where the whole gang is at the craps table, laughing themselves silly and rooting for the dice to hit the number? Great memories.

In the movies, gamblers usually travel in pairs, or solo. You get the great gambling-buddy duos such as Elliott Gould and George Segal in *California Split*, Paul Newman and Tom Cruise in *The Color of Money*, Edward Norton and Matt Damon in *Rounders*, even Jim Sturgess and Kevin Spacey in *21*—but those friendships often fracture or break altogether. Sadly, that happens far too often in real life as well. You get into a dispute with someone over a poker hand, or you have a falling-out with a buddy over a gambling debt, or you refuse to lend money to a pal who's already dropped 10 grand in the first two days of your three-day weekend in Vegas—and it escalates to the point of no return. I've seen it happen with associates, but fortunately, I've never personally experienced the death of a friendship over a gambling-related issue.

Cinematic gamblers who are largely solo artists include Steve McQueen in *The Cincinnati Kid*, Clive Owen in *Croupier*, and of course our man Caan in *The Gambler*. As much as I love the camaraderie of gambling with friends, most of the adventures for this book have been solo journeys. Playing poker online, engrossed in a tournament, buying lottery tickets, or driving to a casino or a track in the middle of a business day—sometimes a man just has to go it alone.

That's why I look forward to the casual home games. Even as I'm in the middle of the 30-day marathon of wagering for the book, I keep playing in my weekly neighborhood games, as well as a couple of monthly tournaments. Oddly enough, I can get away from the gambling by playing in these low-key events. I guess it's like screening movies all day, and yet finding a form of relaxation by clicking around late at night and settling on a 25-minute stretch of a favorite film. You're in a different gear.

You'll hear guys talk about their "poker buddies." It doesn't mean you never hang out with them beyond the felt-covered tables at somebody's house or in the casinos; it means you met these guys through your mutual love of the game, and it remains a common bond. Some of the guys I've met through poker have become close and trusted friends. We go on double dates; we'll get dinner; we'll meet up at a White Sox game; we'll get involved in business ventures together.

But no matter what we're doing, at some point the conversation will turn to the cards.

Over the last three or four years, I've played in at least a hundred hold 'em tournaments online, usually at PokerStars or Full Tilt. You pay an entry fee of $100 or $200 (or you win a seat via satellite), and boom, you're in. No trip to Vegas, no long wait for the next tournament to start. The major tournaments are on Sundays, but each day and every night, there are myriad opportunities to play in tourneys where first prize is worth well over $10,000.

From time to time you'll find yourself at the table with a famous pro, since as I've mentioned, nearly all of the big names have endorsement deals with online sites. You can be a scratch amateur golfer, but you're never going to get the chance to shoot a round in a top tour-

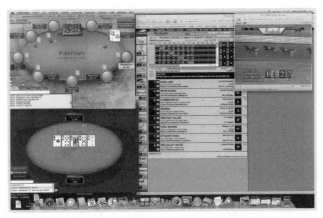

I did a lot of multitasking over the 30 days. Here I'm playing in two poker games while betting the races, all without leaving my computer.

nament with Tiger Woods. You can be an average poker player, and every day there's a legit chance you'll be squaring off against legends of the game such as Phil Hellmuth or Phil Ivey or Doyle Brunson.

According to *Bluff* magazine's online charts, I've won a little more than $112,000 in tournament play over the last couple of years. Of course, that doesn't take into account all the money spent on entry fees—or the dough I've lost in sit 'n' go tournaments (those single-table tournaments in which the top two or three players win cash) or cash games.

Yet I don't feel like I play that much online. There's never been a day when I woke up and said, "I'm going to do nothing but play online poker all day today." (Unlike the thousands of people I mentioned earlier who actually make their living playing online cash games.) When I enter a tournament, it's usually on a weekday night or a winter weekday afternoon. I've got three computers, a satellite radio connection, and a TV monitor in my home office. While I'm playing in a five-hundred-player tournament on a Saturday afternoon, I'm also watching Big 10 football, researching a column, catching up on e-mails, having lunch, making phone calls, and puttering around the house. Only if I'm in a particularly heated hand or I'm deep into the tournament will I focus my full attention on the virtual poker action.

Of course, the hardcore pros love guys like me. We think we're pretty good, but we're not paying attention to our opponents' tendencies, we're not creating a table image, we're not studying hand histories. We look up, see what we have, and bet or fold accordingly. Sometimes we get so distracted we forget to play, and the computer will log us out of the game and we have to click the I'M BACK icon to reenter the action. (I've entered tournaments a few hours in advance and then left the house, forgetting about the action altogether. The next day when I log in, I'll find out I came in 374th out of 515th just by getting blinded off.)

Among my best online tournament finishes:

- 1st out of 213 players in a $50 hold 'em/rebuy tourney: good for $10,771
- 3rd out of 180 players in a $100 no limit hold 'em/rebuy tournament: $7,461
- 4th out of 525 players in a $200 no limit hold 'em/rebuy tourney: $27,424
- 5th out of 665 players in a $150 no limit hold 'em tourney: $5,250
- 6th out of 333 players in a $200 no limit hold 'em/rebuy tourney: $10,746
- 6th out of 223 players in a $100 no limit hold 'em/rebuy tournament: $3,699
- 8th out of 296 players in a $1,000 hold 'em tournament: $8,880
- 8th out of 1,075 players in a $150 no limit hold 'em tourney: $3,628

When I look back on those tournaments, it's a lot easier to recall the hands on which I got knocked out or took a bad beat, as opposed to the lucky suckouts that got me to the final table in the first place. On the other hand, I have no memory of the countless tournaments

in which I never found traction and wound up something like 545th out of 1,650 entrants.

As we've discussed, there are a lot of gray areas when it comes to playing online poker in the United States. Sometimes I can use a credit card or my checking account to directly deposit funds into my account. On other occasions—like today—I have to fund the account via Western Union, either because a particular site doesn't accept credit cards from American customers or because I've reached my deposit limit for the day/the week/the month.

I go to the PokerStars' virtual cashier cage and request instructions for sending cash via Western Union. Within a second, a window pops up on my screen:

> Please use the following information for your transfer:
> Transfer to: Roger Morales Chavarria
> City: San Jose
> Country: Costa Rica
> Please note that some Costa Rican names have a first name and two last names. There are no middle names. Make sure that the receiver's name is spelled exactly as shown above, as we will not be able to confirm the transaction otherwise. . . .
> Once you have sent the money, please return to the Cashier screen to enter your Western Union Control Number (MTCN) to complete this transaction.

Next stop: the currency exchange around the corner. I fill out the proper form,* checking the "Money in Minutes" option to ensure a quick transfer of funds, and get in line with the folks who are renewing licenses, buying CTA bus passes, cashing checks, etc. From behind the bulletproof glass (there's a company called National Bullet Proof, Inc., that specializes in such products), a cheerful clerk does her end

---

* On the front of the Western Union form, it says: "Sending money always makes a PERFECT GIFT. (Enviar dinero siempre es el major regalo.)" Words to live by.

of the paperwork and takes my cash—$300 to be sent to my brand new best friend Roger Morales Chavarria in Costa Rica (plus an $18 service fee). I sign the receipt and get my 10-digit Money Transfer Control Number, and it's back to the home computer, where I log in and fill out step 2, depositing the newly transferred funds into my PokerStars account.

Within about a half hour, the money I sent to Roger Morales Chavarria has now been added to my cash account. I'm good to go! Time to settle back for some online tournament and cash-game action, playing poker with thousands of other men and women who are perched at their laptops and desktops in Belgium, London, New York, Vancouver, Milan, Amsterdam . . .

Day 20

**Bankroll:
−$6,770**

On Final Four weekend in Detroit, there was a lot of fuss and holler in the sports media over a report that at least one student-athlete did a little gambling at one of the downtown casinos:

> DETROIT (AP)—North Carolina guard Ty Lawson has already won big at the Final Four. Don't expect the NCAA to make a commercial about it, though.
>
> Hours after arriving in Detroit, the North Carolina point guard hit a downtown casino and left with a little cash. . . .
>
> "I won about $250 [playing craps]," said Lawson.
>
> "The only time I lost was in Reno; that's when everybody on the team lost," he said. "It's the only place I lost. The other five or six times I did gamble, I won at least $500."

A spokesman for the UNC team noted that Lawson is 21 and said he "was amazed people are going to make a big deal" about the little gambling excursion. Lawson didn't break any NCAA rules, but NCAA president Myles Brand told the Associated Press that gambling is "highly discouraged."

Obviously, you worry about a slippery slope. You'd hate for a great talent like Lawson to go from casual, naive gambler to the next Pete Rose. And any time an athlete displays a voracious appetite for gambling, rumors are sure to swirl about. (Just ask Michael Jordan. To this day there are conspiracy theorists who believe Jordan's first retirement from the NBA was orchestrated by the league so they wouldn't have to suspend him for life for some sort of nefarious gambling-related activities. It should be noted there's never been a shred of evidence to indicate this is anything more than pure urban legend.)

A number of sports pundits are expressing shock and outrage over the very idea of the Final Four taking place in a city where they have casinos. (As if that's Detroit's worst problem.)

"At least Lawson didn't traipse across the Detroit River to Windsor, Ontario, where he could have legally shot craps, bought drinks for teammates as young as 19, bought an all-nude lap dance, and ordered a prostitute," huffed a columnist for *Sports Illustrated*.

I don't know. I'm not encouraging such activities for today's role-model student-athlete, but, gee, a hardened cynic might say that partaking in such activities sounds like a training course for a certain percentage of NBA players.

If a young man is old enough to fight for his country, buy a house, get married, have children, have a drink, and play for a school that rakes in tens of millions of dollars every year from the basketball program, let's not pretend to believe he's going to lose his innocence by shooting craps in a casino.

At least North Carolina coach Roy Williams, who's in the midst of a five-year, $10 million contract with UNC to coach these "amateur" athletes, refused to be a hypocrite on the gambling "controversy." Said Williams: "If we don't want those kids [going to the casinos], don't put the Final Four in a city where the casino is 500 yards from our front door. . . . You know when we got here? Wednesday. I mean, I'm not gonna tell my guys they got to stay in the room and watch Bill Cosby reruns for four days. Come on."

Apparently Williams himself likes to roll the bones.

"When I came here [last fall] to play Michigan State, we stayed at MGM," he said. "And I went down and shot craps and lost—and we won the game. I go to Reno, we play Reno-Nevada, and I stayed in a casino, and I went downstairs and shot craps and lost, and my team won. So you've got to be half-an-idiot if you think I'm not going to go gamble and lose money before this game."

Wait a minute. One of the most acclaimed coaches of his generation thinks there's some kind of rabbit's-foot correlation between him losing at craps and his teams winning basketball games? And he's throwing out "half-an-idiot" comments?

Ah, the world of amateur athletics and all its hypocrisies. Nobody even bothers to mention any more that teams making it to the Final Four play nearly 40 total games in a season, meaning they're on the road more often than Coldplay. Guess they must get excused from class every once in a while.

My online tournament play yielded one small payout, a handful of bad beats, and a net loss. Today I'm turning my attention back to basketball.

As you might recall, after the first weekend of the NCAA tournament, I was 54th out of literally millions of entrants in the CBS online pool.

Heading into the final game, I'm in 265,746th place. Woo. Hoo.

After North Carolina destroyed a tough Michigan State team in Detroit by 25 points early in the season, I was talking basketball with my father and I voiced the opinion that UNC could be the first college team in three decades to go undefeated. (The 1976 Indiana Hoosiers of Scott May, Kent Benson, and my fellow Thornridge High alum Quinn Buckner were the last team to have an unblemished record. The 1991 UNLV team entered the tourney undefeated and was drawing comparisons to the greatest teams of all time, before they lost in the semifinals to Duke.) College teams play about 10 more games in a season these days and the competition is more ferocious, making it nearly impossible to go an entire campaign without stumbling—but UNC looked that dominant early on. And indeed they won their first 14 games before their first loss, against Boston College.

The Tar Heels have been even more impressive thus far in the NCAA tournament. Their closest game has been a 12-point victory over Oklahoma, their average margin of victory has been about 20 points, and they have had the lead in games more than 90 percent of the time overall. There's never been a moment in this tournament when they've been seriously threatened.

UNC's opponent in the championship game tonight: that same Michigan State team they thrashed earlier in the season. But the Spartans have peaked at just the right time and the game is once again at Ford Field in Detroit, meaning they'll enjoy the closest thing to a home-court advantage you can have in the Final Four. (Motivated by pure greed, the NCAA has been staging the Final Four in giant domed arenas instead of traditional basketball stadiums since the late 1990s. Crowds of 70,000 or more pack the rafters. Probably half of the people in attendance need binoculars just to get a good view of the actual game. You'll never see an NCAA championship game played on an actual college campus or even in a pro arena that can seat "only" 23,000.)

About 25 minutes before the final game tips off, I'm walking home from a screening of *Observe and Report* (what a weird effin' movie!) when I dial up Sid's hotline number to see if the lines have changed since earlier in the day. (If there's a lot of action on one side, a bookie might shift the number a bit to balance things out.) Nope. North Carolina is still an 8½ point favorite, and the over/under on total points scored is 152½.

The online sites are offering all kinds of prop bets—largest lead in the game, how many three-pointers UNC will make, total points plus rebounds by Chris Allen, total assists by Ty Lawson—but I'm staying away from the coin-flip craziness tonight and betting the game, the over/under, and a two-bet parlay combining those bets. As I head to the River North area to meet up with a few friends to watch the game, I keep trying to talk myself out of taking Michigan State and the over. I know the Tar Heels are the superior team, but 8½ points just seems like 2 or 3 points too many. And if the Spartans can score just 72 points in the game, I can't lose both bets. A score of UNC 81, MSU 72 would mean I'd lose against the spread but the game would go "over," a score of UNC 80, MSU 72 would mean I'd lose the "over" bet, but I'd win the point-spread wager. What could be easier than rooting for MSU to score 72 points? That's just 36 points per half, 18 points every 10 minutes.

Ah, but what's that buzzing around my consciousness? It's the "opposite theory" rearing its crazy head. Often when the gambler is dead certain a team is going to beat the spread, he or she can't help but stop to ask, *Why? What makes you so sure this is the golden lock of the year? What the fuck do you know anyway!*

The gambler never leads the league in self-esteem.

Years ago, a friend of mine was betting heavily on college and pro football and was on a deadly losing streak. Every weekend for about 10 straight weeks, his losing percentage was 60, 70, 80 percent. You could close your eyes and pick teams and you should be somewhere near 50 percent, right? Perhaps inspired by George Costanza's "opposite" theory on *Seinfeld*, in which the hapless Costanza did everything that felt counterintuitive and found himself on the winning streak of a lifetime, my buddy decided he'd bet against his instincts for the rest of the year. If he were sure the Bears would cover, he'd bet big against the Bears. If he just *knew* the Purdue Boilermakers had no chance of covering against Notre Dame, he'd take Purdue.

For a while it worked, but then he got himself into a mind-set in which he would make his picks, get ready to bet against those picks—

and then wonder if he should go against *those* picks because he was subconsciously adjusting his selections in the first place, knowing he was going to bet against those picks eventually. And yes, my head hurts too at this point.

I'm not going to go against my initial gut feeling tonight. I call Sid's line and put $2,000 on Michigan State and $2,000 on the over, and I parlay the two bets for another $1,000. If Michigan State wins or just loses by 8 or fewer and the combined score is 153 or more, I'll win $6,600 and I'll be just about even for the month. One college basketball game can erase all the losses of the previous 19 days.

There is a scene in *The Gambler* where James Caan is in the bathtub, listening to some college hoops game on a portable radio. (It's 1973. There's no cable TV. No Internet. You're lucky if you can get the game on broadcast TV or AM radio.) He's got a bundle on this game, and it's slipping away. Nothing else matters at this moment to the gambler. He's inside that radio, attached to that moment, despairing at what happens.

I'm in a sports bar with friends, and the UNC-MSU game is playing on dozens of HD monitors, with the sound system blaring the commentary—yet I feel like James Caan locked away in that bathroom, listening to the game on a tinny radio and shutting out all over-stimuli. The only difference is, Caan lost his bet in the final seconds of the game, whereas I'm doomed from the start.

There was a lot of talk—way too much talk—about how the Michigan State Spartans were providing a much-needed boost to the state's beleaguered populace, who have been hit particularly hard by the recession. (You see photo spreads of downtown Detroit, with dogs roaming free and abandoned house after abandoned house, and it looks like a city in wartime.) Even some of the Spartan players are saying they'd really love to win this game and give the people of Michigan something to smile about. As if playing in front of 70,000 fans and a national television audience against one of the most storied programs of all time isn't pressure enough for a 20-year-old.

Not to use that as an excuse. From the opening tip, it's apparent North Carolina is stronger, faster, more talented, and far more poised. It looks like a scrimmage between a varsity team and a JV squad.

Just four minutes into the game, UNC leads 17–7. POW! My cushion, that big, fat, irresistible 8½-point spread, has been erased.

By the time it's UNC 40, Michigan State 12, even the CBS announcers can't pretend Michigan State has a chance at pulling off a miracle comeback. It's still the first half, and they're saying this one's over.

It's not even halftime, but I know I've lost my bet on Michigan State, which means I've also lost my parlay. Breaking even is not an option. I'm just hoping the game goes "over," so I'll lose $1,200 instead of $5,400.

At halftime the score is North Carolina 55, Michigan State 34. The Tar Heels have set an NCAA Finals record for most points scored at halftime—but that doesn't mean my "over" bet is a lock. The 89 total points means we're on pace for 178, well above the target of 152½— but when you have a blowout like this, it means play will get sloppy in the second half, subs will get some court time and they'll be bricking shots all over the place, and coaches won't be stopping the clock in the last five minutes with fouls and free throw opportunities.

Sure enough, the second half sees a much slower pace, though Michigan State helps by trying to get off as many shots as possible, hoping against hope to stage some kind of Motor City Miracle. They actually cut the lead to 14 points with about five minutes left, and though there's still little chance of them actually winning the game, I'm down only 5½ points against the spread. Maybe the Spartans will lose by 7 or 8!

But that's as close as Michigan State can get. If you backed North Carolina tonight, you were in a comfort zone from start to finish.

As for the over/under, there are a few nervous moments as the clock winds down and the scoreboard seems stuck, but when UNC's Ty Lawson makes a free throw with 1:43 left, I'm officially a winner

on that bet. I clench my fist and whisper, "Yes." Somehow a $1,200 loss almost feels like a win.

As the ever-rationalizing gambler likes to say: it could have been worse.

The Fix Is In!

It's amazing how often fans will casually say, "The fix was in on that game," or, "They must have paid the refs a bundle to throw that one." An ump will miss a call and a fan will bellow, "How much they paying you, blue!" A star receiver will drop his third pass of the game and a fan will say, "I wonder how much he bet on the other team."

Sure, sometimes it's just a case of a frustrated fan blowing off steam—but an awful lot of sports fanatics really do believe the networks try to influence the NBA playoffs in favor of high-marquee matchups, and many fans buy into the theory that NFL games and college games can be fixed.

Which makes me wonder: if you think so many games are tainted, how do you even remain a fan?

Then again, hardly a day goes by without another headline about a slugger or a cyclist or a gymnast or a footballer taking an illegal and/or banned substance, so it's hard not to be cynical about things. With all the other trouble surrounding players and officials, why *wouldn't* some of them be susceptible to payoffs?

I've always maintained it would be impossible to come up with enough money to bribe a superstar who's making $15 million a year—but what about the official who might be in financial trouble, or the manager who has a gambling problem, or the long snapper who could mess up a game with one not-so-innocent "mistake"?

It happens. In the late 1970s, infamous mob figure Henry Hill of *Goodfellas* fame got his hooks into a trio of Boston College basketball players who conspired to shave points in nine games. In 1985, five Tulane hoopsters were accused of shaving points. Just a few years ago, former NBA referee Tim Donaghy pleaded guilty to two felony counts of selling inside information to professional gamblers.

In 2009, six former Toledo athletes—three football players and three basketball players—were charged with conspiracy to commit sports bribery. According to the indictments, two gamblers who paid off the athletes made some big bets against Toledo, including $44,000 in a game with St. Bonaventure, $40,000 in a game with Northern Illinois, and $40,000 in a contest with Western Michigan.

Of the 17 basketball games mentioned in the indictment, bettors going against Toledo would have won 11 times. Proof that even when the "fix" is in, it doesn't guarantee victory—especially in a team sport, in which a coach can bench a player who is turning the ball over with alarming regularity or missing easy assignments.

It would be beyond naive to assume there's *never* any cheating going on—but I still believe that in 99 percent of the sporting events on which you can risk money, the players are trying their hardest and the officials are doing their best to get the calls right.

Day 21

**Bankroll:
−$8,000**

Bet with your head, not with your heart.

Bet with your *head*, not with your heart.

It's one of the first rules of gambling.

It's also a rule every gambler breaks all the time. Sure, I believe in the disciplined approach at the poker and blackjack tables, and I try to incorporate common sense into most of my gambling plays—but what's the fun in being a gambler if you're not going to embrace the inconsistencies and say, "Fuck the head, I'm betting with my heart today!"

There are times when you've got to go with your gut instinct—when you triple the size of your blackjack bet, or you make the call in poker even though you've got nothing but third pair, or you bet on a horse because you had a dream about him or her winning. (You remember the dream, yes?)

Going into the adventure, my rules stated I would have to bet at least 25 percent of my bankroll on one event, whether it was a single blackjack hand, a roll of the dice, or a sporting event. Right now I'm down about eight grand, with a few thousand in bets pending—but my starting bankroll was actually about $20,000. (In the journal, I started with the figure of $0 so it would be easier to show whether I was up or down. If I'm down $8,000 and I list my bankroll as $12,000—well, that doesn't seem so bad. I've still got 12 thou! But when you see −$8,000, it hits home. I don't want to be the equivalent of the guy who goes to Vegas with $5,000 in his pocket, sees he has $1,700 remaining on his last night in town and thinks, "Not too bad. I was planning on dropping the whole $5,000, but I've still got $1,700 on me.")

Twenty-five percent of $20,000, that's $5,000. But I'm down some $8,000—so if I'm going to make a big-ass bet, why not go double or nothing? If I win, I'm dead even and I've still got a shot at turning a decent profit for the month. If I lose, I'm down $16,000, and I'll probably devote the rest of the journey to finding long shots—or I'll go the ultraconservative route and play only games where the house advantage isn't too high, trying to cut my losses. (And remember, if I lose more than $15,000 total, I lose an extra $1,000 to my buddy Mel. Fucker.)

There's something liberating about this self-imposed "rule." Instead of facing the uphill battle of trying to grind my way back to the break-even mark, I can reach the surface with a single surge. If you ran a baseball team and you were 10 games out of first, and you were given the opportunity to play one game that would count for 10 games in the standings, either putting you in a tie for the lead or hopelessly behind, wouldn't you jump at the chance? The big bet isn't desperate—the big bet is the product of unbridled optimism! After all this time betting, I still believe.

I'm going to put $8,000 on the White Sox. The minute I say it to myself, it becomes a reality.

Ever since I was a little boy, my favorite sports teams have been ranked thusly:

1. Chicago White Sox
2. Chicago Bears
3. Chicago Bulls
4. Chicago Blackhawks
5. Oakland Raiders
6. UCLA Bruins (basketball)
7. USC Trojans (football)

It really hasn't changed much since then. The Sox are my favorite sports team by a wide margin. (Why yes, thanks for asking: my book about the team, *Sox and the City*, is indeed still available in hardcover and paperback.)

But that doesn't mean the White Sox are my favorite team on which to bet. In fact, I don't have a favorite team against the spread, and as a rule I haven't wagered a whole lot of dough on baseball over the years. (Though I did put a few bucks on the Sox in each game of the postseason in 2005, as well as betting for them to win the World Series.) You'll have a tough time breaking even if you bet football, you'll struggle if you bet basketball—but you'll go broke much faster if your specialty is picking baseball games. Even the best teams lose 60 games a year; even the best pitchers get rocked from time to time. The worst team in baseball beating the best team in baseball on any given day is nowhere as big of an upset as the worst team in basketball or football beating the best in the game. Even when you factor in the spreads, there would be nothing shocking about the Washington Nationals pounding the Los Angeles Dodgers 12–2, beating the spread by 11½ runs. But if the St. Louis Rams beat the Pittsburgh Steelers 50–7—that's a real shocker.

The White Sox are slight favorites over the Royals for the home opener on the South Side of Chicago this afternoon. (The game had been scheduled for Monday, but the weather was so wintry that officials postponed it on Sunday night, thus saving 30,000-plus fans the inconvenience of heading to the park for a game that had no chance of going off.) We've got the steady Mark Buehrle on the mound, but Kansas City is countering with Gil Meche, a pretty tough competitor in his own right. The Royals have been patsies for years, but they're considered to be a team on the rise, while the defending AL Central champion White Sox have been pegged as an uneasy mix of rapidly aging veterans and untested prospects. A year or two ago, the Sox would have been heavy favorites in any home game against the Royals. Now, the oddsmakers are saying this game is nearly a toss-up.

Sid the bookmaker doesn't mind stretching my limits from time to time—but there's no way he's taking $8,000 on a baseball game. He tells me he can handle $2,000 and he can probably lay off another two grand with a couple of other bookies.

No problem. I know a guy who knows another guy who knows a guy. That guy takes $1,500 of my action. The rest can be spread around on the online sites. In less than an hour, I'm down. I've got eight grand on the Sox to win this game straight up. (If I lose, it's going to cost me about $10,000, due to the Sox being slight favorites.)

Outside of the bookmaking world, nobody knows I have this much on the game. When I hook up with some gambling buddies who are tailgating in Parking Lot B beforehand—guys who know about the book and don't flinch at large bets—I tell them I've got quite a bit on the Sox, but for some reason I hint it's a couple of grand, not $8,000. You start talking about $8,000 on a single baseball game, and even guys who wager at a fairly high level will think you're a little bit twisted. It's one thing to enter the multiday Main Event of the World Series of Poker and pay a $10,000 entry fee for the chance to win the first prize of $8 million. It's another thing to risk that much on a single friggin' baseball game on a 40-degree day in early April.

So we joke around in Lot B and we sip Miller Lites as we watch fellow Sox fans playing bean bags. We talk about the prospects for the Sox this year. We catch up on our families and mutual friends. When it's about 15 minutes before game time, my friend and I say our goodbyes to the group and head over to the ball park and my season ticket seats. We greet fellow ticket holders who sit in the same section—familiar faces who have become good friends over the years. Hope springs eternal. If the Sox could do it in 2005, they can do it in 2009! Nobody was picking them to win it all four years ago either.

As long as we're in the sun, it's not a bad day. Hell, it's a *beautiful* day—high blue skies, baseball in the air, the dawn of another summer around the corner. A Marine Corps unit unfurls a gigantic flag that covers the entire infield and half of the outfield, two fighter jets buzz the park, and we all stand for a stirring rendition of "The Star-Spangled Banner." After that, it's the spine-tingling medley of White Sox highlights set to the sounds of "He's a Pirate," followed by the Sox taking the field to the strains of AC/DC's "Thunderstruck." Play ball! Go Sox!

Please, please, please, please, please, please, please. . . .

In the second inning, Alex Gordon of the Royals swings hard and sends a drive to the deepest part of center field. Buehrle drops his head. He knows it's gone. Royals 1, White Sox 0.

Jim Thome starts the bottom of the second for the Sox with a base hit. Jermaine Dye follows with a single, with Thome advancing to second. Paul Konerko rips a single to left—and Thome stops at third.

Bases loaded, nobody out. The near-capacity crowd at U.S. Cellular Field is rocking.

I'm clapping but I'm cursing. I like those big boys in the middle of the Sox lineup, but I swear to you, I can beat two of those three guys out there in a foot race right now. All during the offseason and throughout spring training, the White Sox emphasized they were no longer going to be a lumbering collection of home-run-hitting behemoths. Sure, they'd still hit for power—but the new Sox were going to be faster on the base paths, quicker in the field. You'd see them bunting, stealing bases, taking the extra base.

In reality, they still look like a 16-inch softball team. Three singles and they've yet to get a run in.

A. J. Pierzynski lifts a fly to medium-left field. Thome doesn't even think about tagging up and trying to score. He'd be out by 20 feet.

Bases loaded, one out. We've got a chance to break this game wide open—or it could be the inning I remember as the lost opportunity of the afternoon.

Here's Alexei Ramirez, a.k.a. "the Cuban Missile." He was Mr. Clutch in the stretch last year. Ramirez lifts a fly to left field. The runners cannot advance because the runners are *too slow*.

Bases loaded, two outs. We've been standing for most of the inning, but now most of us are settled back in our seats.

Now batting, Josh Fields.

Crack! Base hit to left! Thome scores and Dye rounds third but they'll hold him up—wait a minute, why are they sending him, he's heading for home . . .

And he's out by a mile and a half, out by so much he doesn't bother to slide. Jermaine bangs into the catcher but fails to jar the ball loose.

Inning over. Four hits, just one run. Game tied at 1–1. One more clutch hit or some speed on the base paths, and it could have been 3–1.

The Royals score again in the top of the fifth to take a 2–1 lead. In the meantime, Meche is mowing down the Sox in rapid fashion. A single here and there, but nothing more. In the seventh, A.J. gets thrown out by 10 feet trying to stretch a single into a double. It's obvious the Sox are pressing, trying to force the situation. They know time is running out.

When the sun goes out of reach, the temperature seems to drop about 20 degrees. Just about everyone in our section layers up with sweatshirts and coats. I'm nursing a beer, shaking my head. They're going to lose 2–1. To the fucking Royals.

After Buehrle departs, White Sox relievers Octavio Dotel and Clayton Richard do a stellar job of holding the Royals to that 2–1 lead. I'm thinking if we can just find a way to tie this thing, we'll win it in extra innings.

First thing we have to do is get Gil Meche out of there—and the Royals answer that prayer by sending out Kyle Farnsworth to start the bottom of the eighth.

"Yes!" bellows a fan in my row. "They put the former Cub in there. It's all over now!"

In addition to the Cubs, Farnsworth has pitched for the Braves and the Yankees, and he's had two stints with the Tigers. He's a six-foot-four, 235-pound fireballing strikeout artist who can still get close to 100 mph on the radar gun—but he's never become the dominant reliever he was projected to be when he first came up. (As of this writing, Farnsworth has a career mark of 31-51, with an ERA of 4.55.) But year after year, he finds a home with another team that's smitten with his raw talent.

Josh Fields, the power-hitting third baseman for the Sox, leads off the inning. *Come on, Josh, take him deep. . . .*

Fields surprises everyone in the park by laying down a beautiful bunt, and he easily reaches first safely. The crowd stirs. Up steps DeWayne Wise, who fails to execute the sacrifice and eventually flies out to center, earning more than a smattering of boos from the fans.

One out, one on.

Chris Getz pokes a single to right and Fields reaches third, and now we're making some serious noise. Tying run just 90 feet away!

Here comes Carlos Quentin, an MVP candidate last year until he broke his wrist in one of the goofiest injuries in White Sox history. The intense Quentin didn't get injured by a pitch or by diving in left field; he broke the bone when he slapped his own bat after missing a pitch.

Still, this is the guy you want at the plate with two on and one out. Even a medium fly ball will be enough to score Fields and tie the game.

Farnsworth reaches back and finds his A-game fastball. Quentin seems overmatched. He goes down swinging. *Fuck.*

They're going to lose this game 2–1. I'm going to look back at the second inning and the eighth inning and lament those lost opportunities. For the Sox, it'll be a disappointing home opener, but they'll shake it off and get ready for the next game in a 162-game season. For me, the sting won't fade any time soon. Ten grand on a goddamn baseball game. So stupid. Bet with your head, not with your heart.

Standing at the plate now is Jim Thome, the country-strong future Hall of Famer from Peoria, Illinois. Is there a classier gentleman in all of baseball?

A typical Thome story for you: At a taping of *Oprah* a few years ago, O pointed out to her viewers that Thome was in the stands with his wife. It was quite a sight: the burly Thome, who looks like a human version of Mr. Incredible, sitting with all those gals in the studio audience. When Oprah asked him why he was here, Thome explained that every year for the past decade and a half, he'd go off to spring training for six weeks while his wife took care of their kids. When he asked her this year if there was anything special he could do for her before he headed to Arizona, the wife said, "Take me to a taping of *Oprah.*" So that's what he did. He's just a cool, decent, regular guy. He's also hit more than 550 home runs without anyone even whispering a rumor about steroid use.

Farnsworth on the mound. Thome at the plate, pointing his bat at Farnsworth and then settling back into his stance.

Farnsworth in the stretch, and he delivers a fastball.

Thome swings—and he launches a high, deep drive to right-center field. At first I think he got under it and it's going to be a warning-track out, but the ball keeps carrying and carrying, deep into that high-blue sky, and when it settles back to earth it is a three-run homer, the most beautiful sight you can imagine. Fireworks explode above the center-field scoreboard as the crowd roars with such gusto I can feel my ears pop. I'm hugging my friend, high-fiving everyone around me, watching Thome as he pumps his fist and rounds the bases. Thome is mobbed by his teammates as he returns to the dugout, and the fans won't let up until he stands on the dugout steps and waves his cap. It is an electric moment. I'm exhaling as if I've just finished a four-mile run.

Sox 4, Royals 2.

Of course, the game isn't over. After the Sox are retired, Bobby Jenks takes the mound for the Sox in the ninth and quickly strikes out Coco Crisp, but then David DeJesus singles to left center, putting the tying run at the plate. It's never easy.

Teahan flies to right. Two down. Fans on their feet, roaring.

Jose Guillen at the plate. He's got home-run power. The Royals are still just a home run away from making it 4–4.

Jenks fires, Guillen swings—and lifts a harmless fly ball to center field. This ball game is *ovah*. Sox 4, Royals 2.

There was never any doubt in my mind.

Day 22

**Bankroll:
Even!**

A man *grows tired of selfish things. It is 10 P.M., and he realizes that
since he awoke at 6 this morning, he has not thought of anything
but gambling.*

Over the last 21 days, the man has wagered literally hundreds of
thousands of dollars on more than a dozen games of chance and skill.
Is anyone a better person when he is gambling than when he is not
gambling?

All day long today, he has played poker online and he has bet on
ponies racing in circles at tracks around the country. He has fired off
bets of as much as $1,200 on a single hand of cards, and as much as
$400 on single horse race. He was up and down, up and down, up and
down—and now, late in the evening, he is ahead quite a bit. He takes a
break to check e-mails and text messages and phone calls, to check on
Twitter and Facebook and his personal Web site, and there he finds all
these little life updates from friends and family and readers, all these

people who spent the day working and going to school and spending time with their families and interacting with the world.

The man hasn't done any of that. He grabbed some coffee just after dawn and he grilled a little lunch at midday, but other than that he has been attached to the computers all day and all night, betting and betting and betting, thinking of nothing else but the next hand of poker or the next race in Pennsylvania or New York or California or wherever the hell it might be.

Enough. The man grabs a fistful of cash and heads into the city, and he starts walking.

Within a block, he encounters a man sitting on a bucket. The man asks him for some spare change—and he hands the man a $20 bill.

A half-block later, a similar scenario.

The man keeps walking, looking for people who have less than nothing. It's not hard to find them.

He keeps handing out $20 bills. Maybe it's a little crass. Maybe it's a little condescending. Maybe it's an empty gesture. He doesn't think this means he's a great person or even a good person—in fact, it almost feels tacky in its obviousness. He's just doing it because it seemed like he needed to do **something** positive to offset the day-draining, utterly selfish way in which he just spent the last 14 hours.

After a while, the man heads home. The horses are still running in Australia.

Days 23–24

Bankroll:
+$1,400

One of the organizers of the Be There 4 Bill fundraiser calls and tells me I'm one of the $1,000 winners in the raffle, which means I broke even on that particular "bet." She says they'll be sending out a check in the next couple of days.

Of course, I tell her to put a stop on that check. There is no way I'm taking $1,000 back from a family trying to cope with the loss of a husband and father.

This doesn't mean I'm Mr. Magnanimous. Hell, if I'd won the grand prize I would have gladly accepted the bulk of it, thank you very much. But in the interest of karma alone, I'm not taking that grand.

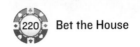

Poker players can't help themselves. They have to tell their bad beat stories. They realize nobody gives a shit about these stories—and they tell 'em anyway.

In the men's room during the break in any poker tournament, that's all you'll hear: one bad beat story after another, overlapping, never-ending, blah-blah-blah-de-fucking-blah.

The stories are all different but they're all the same. It all comes down to: "I had the best hand and I played it perfectly, and this dipshit donkey at the table had a worse hand and he played it like an idiot— and then he got lucky on the river and beat me. Can you believe it?"

Yes, I can believe it. Because it happens *all the time*.

Here's the difference between, say, the World Series of Poker and baseball's World Series. In the latter, luck may play a small factor in the form of a fortuitous bounce of the ball or an umpire's bad call, but the winning team usually gets there by virtue of hitting, pitching, and fielding. Skills.

In the World Series of Poker, the full-time pros will of course play better over the long run than the semipros and the rank amateurs— but it doesn't necessarily mean they're going to win any given tourney. As Phil Hellmuth will tell you, if luck didn't play into it, he'd win every tournament. The last several Main Events of the World Series of Poker have been won by amateurs or semiprofessionals. In order to outlast a field of eight thousand or more players, you are going to have to win at least a dozen hands in which you were the underdog at some point in the hand. You're going to have to get lucky by hitting a miracle King on the river.

The best starting hand in Texas hold 'em is pocket Aces. The worst starting hand is 7-2 off-suit. The Aces will beat the 7-2 about 87 percent of the time—but that still means the 7-2 will "suck out" and win 13 percent of the time. Poker is a game of skill and in the long run the pros will separate the amateurs from their money—but in every tournament, the amateur has a legitimate chance. He's never going to hit a double off Tim Lincecum or sack Peyton Manning, but he can beat the best professional poker players in the world on a national stage.

Talk about a bad beat. A guy goes all-in with Jack-4 against my Ace-King and gets incredibly lucky. Note my typed reaction in the chat box.

Luck is a factor. Bad beats happen. We all bitch about them.

What we don't talk about nearly as much are the "good beats"— i.e., winning hands that should have been losers.

I'm playing in a $5–$10 cash game on Bodog.com. A player named "Duffman99" raises to $30. I'm in the small blind, meaning I've already put in $5, but I have one of the worst starting hands in poker: 8-4. Pure garbage. I should fold, but I feel like playing, so I call. No other reason. I just feel like playing.

Now I don't know this during the hand, but it turns out Duff-man99 has an Ace-8. In poker parlance, I'm "dominated." Duffman99 is a 72 percent favorite at this point.

The flop comes 8-5-4. Gold for me. I get two pair, but Duffman99 has top pair with top kicker. He has to think he has the best hand, unless I went in with something like 7-6 and flopped a straight.

Duffman99 bets $75.

I raise it to $200.

Duffman99 goes all-in for the rest of his cash, exactly $672.

I call instantly.

The turn is 9, the river is a 10, giving no help to Duffman99 and giving me the pot. I rake in more than $1,500 on a single hand, just because I felt like playing that garbage hand of 8-4. If you're Duffman99, you're thinking: what is this idiot doing? Why is he calling with 8-4? How could his moronic play get rewarded with that flop?

Bad beat for Duffman99. Good beat for me.

My father quite possibly has never placed a bet in his life. Same with my mother.

My brother likes to play poker on a casual level. My older sister enjoys miniexcursions to the boats in Indiana and Michigan, where she and her husband play the slots and other games for reasonable stakes. My younger sister isn't much into gambling.

It's not like I grew up in one of those households where the grownups were always playing cards at the kitchen table and the folks regularly jetted off to Vegas. (In fact, they never jetted off to Vegas.) When the parents and the aunts and uncles and grandparents did play cards, it was gin rummy or a little poker for penny stakes.

So where the hell does this gambling habit of mine come from?

Then again, why do I drink more Stella Artois than my doctor would find advisable? Why is my head turned so quickly by a beautiful woman? Why do I sprint every morning for that first coffee? Why do I work so many hours and take on so many jobs? Why do I indulge in so many activities and habits that would be deemed troublesome by most normal folks?

It's because I can't sit still. I don't sleep more than four or five hours most nights. I find that life is alternately too beautiful to bear and too mundane to endure.

Because I love the chase more than I love winning. Because I can compartmentalize. Because my idea of "discipline'" is to selfishly live a life of doing what I want to do when I want to do it, as long as I balance the equation with productive work, quality family time, and doing just enough charity work and other good-deed shit to assuage my guilt and convince myself I'm a good guy who does the right thing more often than not.

But what about the gambling? On some level I'm addicted to it—yet I can turn it on and off for years at a time. (That's what they all say, right?)

I gamble because I can. Because I'm often able to set my own schedule for the day, giving myself pockets of time to indulge this habit or that habit or even that other habit. Because I've often had extra cash that didn't have to go toward tuition or anything else normal people my age would be spending on their kids—because I've never been married and I don't have kids. Long after two perpetual Peter Pans and personal pop-cult heroes of mine, Jerry Seinfeld and David Letterman, finally settled down and had families, I'm still out there living the clichéd life of the eternal bachelor.

Recently I met up with a former girlfriend who is now happily married with two children. She is such a good soul. She went on and on about how she wants me to meet the right person, just as she finally did. She wants this for me so I can know true happiness, so I can have children of my own. I appreciated everything she said (and in fact I've never ruled out marriage and children). But she is under the mistaken impression that my life is on hold waiting for my *real* life to begin. She thinks I'm unhappy or in denial, and she couldn't be more wrong. Unhappy *sometimes*, yes, of course. If you don't feel the darkness once in a while, you're a cartoon character. But I wouldn't have the balls to be unhappy on a regular basis, not with the life I've been dealt. How dare someone like me complain. It would be obscene.

Here's the other thing about gambling: it's fucking *fun*. Not always, and by now you've seen me hit the wall from all the grinding away—but most of the time, even now, it's a hell of an entertaining thing. There's a high you get every time you sit down for a session of blackjack or you start a poker tournament. Maybe it's not healthy, maybe it's not morally admirable—but it's there, especially on days

when I'm getting the right cards, picking the right teams, making the right picks on the races.

Just because I don't believe in streaks doesn't mean I'm not on one damn hot streak right now.

Days 25-28

Bankroll:
+$4,200

"The night before I left Las Vegas I walked out in the desert to look at the moon. There was a jeweled city on the horizon, spires rising in the night, but the jewels were diadems of electric and the spires were the neon of signs ten stories high."
—*Norman Mailer*

On day 21, I was down $8,000 and looking at a bankroll of –$18,000—and then with one mighty swing, Jim Thome turned it all around.

Now I'm back in Las Vegas, for blackjack and poker. No gimmick games on this trip. No forays into the high-limit slots area. No roulette, no keno, no sports bets, no video poker, no baccarat.

I'm not here to gamble. I'm here to win.

If I can win a few thousand in the cash games, make a run or two at the blackjack tables and cash in the tournament, I could be up $15,000 or $20,000 by the time I head back to Chicago.

I've been to Las Vegas about a hundred times over the last 25 years.

If I listed the top 50 and the worst 50 days of my life, Vegas would be the locale for five or six of the top days—and at least three or four of the worst.

I have had insane fun and I have experienced freefalling, dangerous lows in various gleaming casinos on the Strip. I've fallen in love—and I've fallen into hellacious fights—in tiny hotel rooms and in rock star suites. There was one night at the Venetian when I was sure nobody on the planet was having a better time, and that's probably all I should say about that.

Some of the friends with whom I shared early crazy-bonding Vegas moments have long ago left the gaming tables and have left my life; it takes me a moment to remember all the names. Other friends—longtime, lifetime friends—are still up for a trip to Vegas once every year or two. We'll find ourselves at the Wynn or the Bellagio or Mandalay Bay—some hotel that didn't exist when we first started coming out here—and we'll shake our heads and wonder, Where the hell did the time go? Wasn't it just the other day that we were a bunch of guys in our 20s, hanging at Caesars Palace or Bally's or the Flamingo, laughing our asses off at the $10 blackjack tables?

In recent years I've become close friends with a whole new bunch of guys who like to play cards, and we're already starting to pile up the Vegas stories that we'll be referencing when we're too old to make it across the floor at the Rio without an oxygen tank and a nurse.

Some of the women with whom I once shared a Vegas weekend are long since married. A few have children who are old enough to make a trip to Vegas on their own. Some of these women are still in my life, as good friends. A few would probably curse my name if it ever comes up, but I doubt it ever comes up.

There was one woman I gladly would have married at any point during about a five-year stretch in my life, had she ever been free of the drama that seemed to follow her around with the relentlessness and the darkness of a shadow. She moved from city to city while I stayed in Chicago; Las Vegas became our meeting point. We had some fantastic times at the Bellagio and Caesars Palace—magical weekends, as if we were in a movie. At least that's how I choose to remember it.

The last time I saw her, it was a Friday night in Las Vegas, many years ago. I'd already been in town a day; she had just arrived. I picked her up at the airport—you've got to be crazy about someone if you pick her up at the Vegas airport after you've already been in town for a day—and brought her to our hotel suite, and after she put away her things we headed to the Hard Rock for a drink. Within an hour, as I was regaling her with some story about my adventures to date, she cut me off and gave me a look that was pure daggers.

"Stop it," she said.

Stop what?

"Stop trying so hard," she told me. "You're trying too hard to be funny. You're trying too hard to be charming. You're trying too hard to make everything perfect every time we come out here. You're overly nice. You've got too much energy. By the time I wake up in the morning, you're already out getting coffee for us. When I nap, you go do something and then you come back and tell me all about it. I can't take it any more. You're wearing me out."

I'm wearing you out? After two hours?

"I don't want this any more," she said. "It's too hard to come out here once a year and live this fantasy. And that's all it is—a fantasy. It just makes it harder for me to go back."

It got worse after that. Much worse. She told me every single thing that was wrong with me, and she mentioned a few other faults I'm pretty sure don't apply to me or even to some of the midlevel terrorists of the world. I eventually snapped out of my state of shock and started fighting back. We forgot about the concert we were supposed to attend and we pushed our drinks aside and kept going at it, finally leaving the Hard Rock and returning to our suite, where the verbal theatrics escalated and we finally reached the point where there was

no going back, no undoing what had been said. No time out. No "I'm sorry" big enough to cover it.

Las Vegas is a terrible place for a relationship to die.

When I offered to leave the suite to her and get out of town, she jumped at it. I called the airlines until I found the next available flight to Chicago, leaving Las Vegas at 6 A.M. Then, as she locked herself in the bathroom, I packed my bag and headed out the door.

There's nothing so headache-inducing as landing in Chicago on a sunny Saturday morning after having a horrific, drawn-out argument in Vegas followed by a sleepless four-hour flight punctuated by countless Bloody Marys.

That was about seven years ago. I never saw her again. We exchanged two or three pleasant but formal e-mails about five years ago. Nothing after that. Don't know where she's living. I've heard enough to know the drama of her life has not faded.

After that terrible fight, I took a break from Vegas. I couldn't imagine landing at McCarran without the memories of that night smacking me right in the face. It was about two years before I'd return.

It's funny, though. Now I can go to the Hard Rock or return to the hotel where I was staying that weekend and hardly hear a whisper of that long-ago night. For all I know I've stayed in that very same suite where we ripped each other's hearts out. And now it's just another suite. Time doesn't heal all wounds so much as it makes you numb to the memory of those wounds.

One of the most successful and often-quoted advertising slogans of the first part of this century was "What happens in Vegas, stays in Vegas." It then morphed into one of the most hackneyed and most overused cliches of the first part of this century.

Obviously it was effective—but it's bullshit. What happens in Vegas doesn't stay in Vegas—it shows up on your credit card statement the next month, and it stays with you for the rest of your days.

Las Vegas is not a place without consequences. (In *The Hangover*, the great Jeffrey Tambor says to his future son-in-law, "What happens in Vegas stays in Vegas. Except for herpes. That shit'll come back with you.")

That said, it *is* a place where some people do things they'd never do anywhere else, whether it's betting ridiculous amounts of money on the draw of a card or the spin of a wheel, chatting or otherwise getting to know young women who provide services for cash, or getting so shit-faced they're *thisclose* to making a trip to the emergency room.

The artifice of Las Vegas never ceases to amaze. All these mega-casinos that are the architectural equivalent of hip-hop music—sampling the original material, co-opting the culture. How many millions of people have been to Paris Las Vegas, but not to Paris, France? How many tourists have snapped pictures of the ⅝-scale imitation of the Eiffel Tower on the Strip? (The original plans were to make the Vegas Eiffel Tower a full-size twin of the original, but it was too close to the airport, so they had to scale it down.)

A few months after September 11, I was looking up at the Statue of Liberty. I could see the Chrysler Building. In another direction, there was the Brooklyn Bridge. Boats bearing the logos of the New York City Fire Department were near the Statue of Liberty. On and near a railing rimming the water near the statue, there were T-shirts, hats, signs, flowers, candles, hand-written notes—all paying tribute to the fallen heroes of September 11. It was all very heartfelt, all very touching.

But it was also more than a little strange, because I wasn't in New York City—I was on Las Vegas Boulevard, at the New York–New York casino complex.

OK, so Las Vegas has casinos with themes based on the cultures of Paris, Rome, Monte Carlo, Egypt, the South Seas—but a casino based on modern-day New York? I never quite got that. It's not as if you can't just as easily fly to, you know, the real New York. Not that it's a stupid idea; the casino has been quite successful since opening in 1997. Evidently a lot of people would rather experience a faux New

York with slot machines than the real thing. (The casino even has its own version of New York's famous Coyote Ugly Saloon. You can enter via a shopping mall.)

First-time visitors to the Strip are inevitably stunned by the sheer hugeness of the casinos and the hotels. As of 2008, a worldwide ranking of the hotels with the largest number of rooms:

1. The Venetian/Palazzo Megacenter, Las Vegas: 7,128 rooms
2. First World Hotel, Malaysia: 6,118
3. MGM Grand, Las Vegas: 5,034
4. Wynn/Encore, Las Vegas: 4,750
5. Luxor, Las Vegas: 4,408
6. Mandalay Bay/THEhotel, Las Vegas: 4,332
7. Ambassador City Jomtien, Thailand: 4,219
8. Excalibur, Las Vegas: 4,008
9. Bellagio, Las Vegas: 3,993
10. Circus Circus, Las Vegas: 3,774

Eleven more Las Vegas hotels are in the top 30. All the great metropolises of the world, all the cities brimming with history and culture and amazing sights and sounds—and most of the world's largest hotels have been built within the last few decades on a single four-mile strip of road in Nevada.

When the gleaming, green-glass MGM opened in 1993, it boasted of having the largest number of hotel rooms in the world. Some five thousand balloons were released at the grand opening, each containing a coupon good for a one-night stay at this latest version of the MGM. They had a whole Emerald City thing going on, with myriad exhibits and themes based on *The Wizard of Oz*, which I always thought was a strange theme for a casino. A gay nightclub, yes—but a gambling emporium? (You might recall that in *Swingers*, when Vince Vaughn and Jon Favreau meet a couple of babes in Vegas, one of them was working as "a Dorothy" at the MGM.) The main entrance to the MGM Grand was a lion's mouth—a touch that kept many of the top

Asian gamblers from entering the casino, as they believed that to walk into a lion's mouth was bad luck. After five years, the big lion's mouth was gone. Eventually the MGM Grand got rid of all the Oz-themed attractions. They also dumped the theme park they had built during Vegas' ill-fated attempt to become more family-friendly.

Vegas always adapts.

The mood at the MGM Grand was anything but family-friendly in November 1996, when Mike Tyson and Evander Holyfield faced off in a long-awaited heavyweight battle. On the night before the fight, the casino was jam-packed with high rollers, including a few young men in gold-plated wheelchairs. (I was told the young men had been paralyzed in street shootings.) Tyson had signed a six-fight contract with the MGM Grand after he was released from prison. At the age of 30, and having served four years of hard time, Tyson wasn't the awesome machine he'd been in his early 20s—but he was still considered to be the best heavyweight in the world, and he was a huge favorite over Holyfield, who was 34 and appeared to be on the verge of retirement after one last big payday. Holyfield had lost three of his previous seven fights, and was such a big underdog that in a poll of 50 boxing writers, only one picked him to win. Pay-per-view customers were actually charged by the round so they wouldn't feel ripped off if the fight lasted only three or six minutes, as many predicted would happen.

Tyson opened as a 25-1 favorite, but a funny thing happened: people kept betting on Holyfield. The odds dropped to 10-1, 8-1, 6-1. As one oddsmaker explained, the average medium-strength bettor wasn't going to risk $100 on Tyson to win $10. But hey, why not take a leap of faith on Holyfield at $100?

I've been fortunate enough to witness a number of major sporting events in my time, including World Series games, the NBA Finals, NCAA tournament action, NFL postseason action, and much more. I've never experienced anything more electric than the atmosphere in the arena that night in November, with 16,000-plus fans (including dozens of A-list celebrities, from Jack Nicholson and Dennis Hopper to Magic Johnson and Steve Martin) standing and roaring through-

out much of the fight. In the early rounds Tyson took the fight to Holyfield, looking to end the thing early with one big punch. But Holyfield stood his ground, scoring with hooks and uppercuts and using his height and reach advantage to keep Tyson at bay.

By the middle rounds, it was apparent an upset could be in the works. In the sixth, Holyfield nailed Tyson with a combination that sent Tyson sprawling across the canvas like a cartoon character as the arena erupted. Tyson managed to stagger to his feet, but he took a beating over the next several rounds and seemed almost relieved when the ref waved off Holyfield in the 11th round and declared a TKO.

I'll never forget the sight of Tyson at the post-fight press conference in a tent outside the arena, wearing a dapper suit but holding a towel against his forehead, as he was still bleeding. He looked humbled and subdued as he shook hands with Holyfield and said, "I have nothing but the greatest respect for you." Who could have imagined that in their next meeting in the ring, Tyson would be acting like a lunatic, biting off a chunk of Holyfield's ear?

Even with the odds on the fight down to 5-1, sportsbooks took huge hit for the night—several million dollars all told. "It was probably the worst disaster in Vegas sports book history," said longtime boxing oddsmaker Herb Lambeck. "It was a bloodbath."

In more ways than one.

As many times as I've been to Vegas, I wouldn't classify myself as a "Vegas guy." Las Vegas is a town that runs on comps and connections and tips and favors—and though I know how those things work, it's never been my thing. I hate the endless ritual. I hate that I have to figure out who to tip in order to get a cabana, and who to schmooze to get a better room, and who's in charge of dinner reservations at the four-star restaurant that's booked three months in advance.

I know. You get the right casino host and they'll take care of all of that for you and much more. That's what I'm told. I've gone that route a few times, and it's like you've hired someone to be your friend. Sometimes it's worked out great; other times, it was more hassle than it was worth.

Nor am I trying to be disingenuous about the very minor level of TV fame I've experienced over the last decade. Yes, it helps open doors, though I'm never going to be the type of guy who walks up to the person standing at the velvet rope to announce, "Do you know who I am?" (If you have to say that, the answer is probably "Uh, no.") Besides, in Vegas, they're used to dealing with Tiger Woods and Michael Jordan, Ben Affleck and Leonardo DiCaprio, Clooney and Pitt. Think they give a shit?

They're also more interested in the anonymous "whale" from Japan or New Jersey than the average star. If you're famous and you want the best suite and it's available, you might get it. If you're a high roller and you're going to risk a couple of million at the baccarat tables, you *will* get it. Hell, they'll kick the president of the United States out of the Presidential Suite if a $10-million-a-weekend gambler is flying in. In Vegas, it's not who you are—it's how much you bet.

When I first started going out there in the late 1980s and really through the 1990s, most of the celebrities you'd see in Vegas were probably working there, or were in town for a big event like a Mike Tyson fight. Even in the *Swingers* era of the late 1990s, you didn't see a lot of Hollywood types or big-name athletes everywhere. The real stars in Vegas were the used-car king from Florida playing blackjack at $500 a hand, the dry cleaning millionaire from Cleveland blowing $20,000 a night at the craps tables, the insurance magnate from Arizona with a heavy slots habit. Those were the guys I'd see getting treated like royalty by the pit bosses and the casino managers. Those were the guys who could get dinner reservations or tickets to the hottest show with a snap of their fingers. Those were the guys with the reserved section at the topless pool.

But over the last half dozen years, Vegas has become achingly hip and upscale trendy, with every major casino in town hosting multiple top-tier restaurants and of course the obligatory megaclub, where

Paris Hilton dances on the tables, Samantha Ronson spins music, and the cast of *Gossip Girl* parties next to Jamie Foxx and his friends.

A funny thing happens nearly every time a cab driver or a black-jack dealer or a cocktail waitress figures out I'm that guy who did that show about the movies. They immediately tell me about the much more famous person they encountered just last week.

"Oh yeah, you're the guy that came on after Siskel," says the cab driver. "I used to catch your show from time to time. It was OK. Hey, you know whom I gave a ride to the other night? Brad Garrett! Man, is he tall."

That's not a hypothetical. It's a near-verbatim quote from a cabbie I had in the summer of 2008.

But even with all the stars who descend on Vegas every weekend, the real celebrities are still the major players. The casinos will take a whale over a well-known any day.

I am not a whale. When my main game was blackjack, I was a fairly big player—Maybe $250 or $300 per hand, with an average of three or four hours per day. Add to that an hour or two of craps, and I was gambling enough to get an RFB comp. (That would be Room, Food, Beverage.) Maybe even a suite instead of a standard room, plus a couple of tickets to a show and a good table at any restaurant in town.

On a few trips, I've hardly gambled at all. I was in Vegas once to give a speech and to spend some time with a woman who had less than zero interest in gambling, but an outstanding level of interest in shopping, dining, *Mamma Mia!* and Cirque du Soleil. I'm not sure I ever placed a single bet for the weekend. You can believe the casino didn't so much as cut a Toblerone candy bar from the minibar from my bill. (Note: In the old days, even the best Vegas hotel rooms didn't have minibars. They wanted you out of the rooms and into the casi-nos. Now, with maybe half of all Vegas visitors of the nongambling variety, the best suites have minibars, 24-hour room service, first-run movies on the flat-screen, and spa services available in your room at the touch of a button.)

When I'm in Vegas strictly to play poker, the comp interest level in me isn't much higher. If I'm grinding it out in a tournament for two straight days, they're getting about $5 an hour from me, if that. Sure, they're happy to have me out there, and I might get one night out of three comped because I'm a regular customer—but they liked me better when I was betting big at the blackjack tables and there was a chance I'd drop $5,000 or $10,000. Contrary to popular myth, you don't get perks based on how much you've lost on a particular trip; you get comped based on your promise to gamble at a certain level. Win or lose, they'll take care of you. They know if you continue to wager at that level, you're eventually going to lose. Maybe not this time out—but eventually.

I've seen players at the blackjack table talking about how they have to get in two more hours of play before the wife meets them for dinner because they've got to meet the minimum time required to justify their comps. Let's say they're staying in a $500-a-night suite and they're racking up another $200 in food and beverage. That's $2,100 in perks for a three-day weekend. Not bad—but this guy will be playing for $500 a hand! He could win or lose that much in less than two minutes. Yet if he drops $24,000 over the weekend, he'll still be bragging to his friends that he was "comped for the weekend," as if that somehow brought him close to even.

Even if you're not a high roller, you can work the Vegas scene. Slip $100 to the right guy down at the pool and he'll see that your name magically moves up to the top of the waiting list for cabanas. (A friend of mine did this once, and within 15 minutes we were hanging next door to Pamela Anderson and Tommy Lee and their tattoos.)

I'm no good at that kind of thing. Never have been and never will be. It all just seems so . . . cheesy.

And yet that's the way Vegas has always worked, and it's the way it works to this day.

I'm in the big blind in a cash game. Guy on the button raises. They always raise on the button. The assumption is the small blind and the big blind probably won't have good hands—so why not just go ahead and raise it and take it?

Then if the big blind raises, the button thinks the big blind is trying to resteal, and he'll reraise.

That's exactly what happens here. I wake up to a pair of Kings in the big blind, and I raise the guy back, and he raises me, and I raise him back, and now there's more than $2,500 in the pot. Turns out he has A-J off-suit, meaning I'm a 71 percent favorite.

Until he spikes an Ace on the turn and cracks my pocket Kings.

"Why would you risk all that money on Ace-Jack?" I say to the guy as he rakes in the huge pot. "What did you think I had, Ace-10? A pair of 9s?"

"I thought you were making a move," he says. Whatever the hell that means. They always say that: I thought you were making a move.

"Unbelievable," I say. "Nobody plays smart poker any more."

I'm starting to sound like one of "those guys." So I take a deep breath and just shake my head.

Another player at the table says, "You can't have it both ways. You want him to make that call. Then he makes the call and you complain when he gets lucky."

"I know," I say. "You're right, you're right. He makes calls like that all day, we'll get all his money."

It gets worse. I get into a hand with 10-7 and I flop two pair—and I'm against a guy who has pocket 10s. I'm drawing dead.

On the very next hand, I make a big move with a flush draw but come up empty. In three hands I've dropped more than $2,000.

Next I enter a tournament with about six hundred players, but instead of playing my usual solid and tight/aggressive game, I try to steal some pots and build a chip stack. It works, and I make it to the final hundred. But then I go card-dead, and with the blinds and antes rapidly escalating, I go all-in with K-8 of hearts and run smack into A-K.

In four separate blackjack sessions over two days, I'm never up more than $500 at any given moment. I'm hanging in there, playing virtually every hand strictly by the book, but for every three hands I win, I lose four.

At night, when most of the rooms are empty and most of the tourists are downstairs in the casino or at dinner or a show or one of the clubs, I'm up in my room, playing cash games online. I didn't bring anyone with me on this trip; I'm here on business. As much as they say they understand that I'm here for poker and blackjack and they'll be perfectly fine shopping and going to the spa and lounging at the pool and seeing me in the evening, there's usually a moment when my companion will show up at the gaming tables and say, "Don't you want to take a break? Can you *please* take a break?"

The online action is brutal. I lose in sit 'n' gos. I lose in the cash games. At one point I lose eight out of nine heads-up matches at $230 a game. If you just pressed the all-in button every time in every game, you'd win two or three out of nine.

Back in the casino, another live tournament. What a collection of players at my table. One guy seems to be channeling Justin Timberlake, from his fedora to his wardrobe to his manner of speech. There's an Italian guy to my right who sees every flop, and I mean every flop. An Asian man, a 60ish woman, a Frenchman who keeps getting up to see how his friends at the other tables are doing, an old-timer with a white ponytail. Also at the table: a friend of mine. There are two-hundred-plus players in this tourney, and by the luck of the draw we're sitting three seats apart.

When Ponytail gets knocked out, a beefy man in a sweat suit takes his place, to my immediate left. He sits down talking, he stacks his chips talking, he plays his hands talking, and even when he's not in a hand he's talking. He's one of those guys who think everything that happens to them is fascinating, and nothing that happens to

you is interesting enough for them to shut up. After nearly every hand he says something like, "That's nothing. This one time I was in a tournament . . ."

He actually tells this joke: "How come men can't get mad cow disease? Because we're pigs." As if to prove it, he leers at every woman under 70 who comes within 20 feet of our table. Please, please, somebody knock this guy out of the tourney.

About two hours into the action, my friend makes a big bet and everyone folds except the Italian. The flop comes 5-7-8. My buddy makes a big bet, the Italian goes all-in, my buddy calls and turns over pocket kings. The Italian? He had 6-4, which means he had no business being in the hand in the first place—but it also means he's flopped a straight, and my buddy is gone.

The Talking Machine immediately launches into a story: "That reminds me of this time when . . ."

I ignore him and tell my buddy I'll catch up with him later. The Talking Machine isn't fazed; after my friend leaves, he just starts the story all over again.

In as friendly a manner as possible, I tell the guy he's got to give me a break. "Unless your next story involves somebody getting killed or a guest appearance by Megan Fox, can you give it a rest for just a bit? I'm sorry, but you're making it hard for me to concentrate."

"I'm sorry, man," he says—and then I swear to you, he just keeps on talking.

With 9-8 off-suit in the small blind, I limp in against Sir Talkalot. He raises. Out of nothing but frustration, I raise back—and he calls.

The flop comes 8-7-2 of spades. I've got top pair with a weak kicker and no flush draw. I bet. He raises all-in. Against my better instincts, I call.

Turns out he has Ace-Jack of hearts. Just two overcards with no flush draw. The turn is a blank and the river is an 8, giving me a set and sending him away from the table. It's the best feeling I've had in three days.

I start getting some strong hands, and those hands are hitting. Players keep calling me down, because that's what players do in the modern era of poker—they call the raise or they raise the raise. They're so addicted to pot odds and implied pot odds that they can talk themselves into playing just about any two cards. They're probably not going to win a tournament unless they get extremely lucky, but they can end *your* tournament with their loose and aggressive play.

With about 28 players left, I'm probably about 7th or 8th in chips—but then my Ace-King gets cracked by an Ace-Queen, and my pocket Queens run into pocket Kings, and all of a sudden I'm short-stacked. The next time I see an Ace, I push all-in and I get a call from a player with King-Queen.

The Ace holds up.

A while later I get Ace-King and go all-in, and I get a caller who has a pair of 9s. I get a King on the flop and another King on the turn.

I'm in the big blind and the player on the button goes all-in with a very small stack. Even though I've got 8-3, I have to call. He has Ace-Jack. I get a three on the flop, an 8 on the turn, and a 3 on the river. That garbage 8-3 turns into a full house.

Another time it's my A-6 against an A-10. The flop comes 3-4-7, I miss the turn—but I draw a 6 on the river. We're down to about 20 players, and I have a healthy chip stack again.

Then I push with Q-Q, and the big blind insta-calls, turning over K-K. Just like that, I'm out of the tournament.

I'm playing strong poker. I'm playing strategically sound blackjack.

And I'm losing. In 72 hours I give back everything I've won in recent days, and then some.

Days 29–30

**Bankroll:
–$2,350**

L ike a bloated cruise ship patron hitting the buffet station one more time on the last day of a long excursion, I try to hit every possible betting station one final time as the adventure winds down.

But I also feel like the vacationer who returns home sunburned and exhausted, having piled up a huge credit card bill. Even as he's plopping down his bags and thinking about how great it will be to sleep in his own bed tonight, he's also wishing he could head straight back to the airport and spend another two weeks in the Bahamas. How soon before we go back?

I'm home now, and I've got a few grand spread out on baseball, the NBA, and the NHL. I monitor my bets while I'm playing in online cash games and making bets on horse races across the country. Things are not going well. With the experiment coming to a close and the bankroll in the red, I try to make a quick kill by betting long shots at the races. Here's a flash: most long shots are long shots for a reason.

My horses are coming in 5th, 7th, 9th, 11th. I don't come close to hitting any of my exactas or trifectas.

When I take a break from the online action, I walk over to the 7-Eleven and buy a fistful of lottery tickets, and then I hit the Stretch Run OTB and bet on the next five races available. I don't even bother buying a program or checking the track conditions. I just take the #1 horse to win all five times, and I pair the #1 with the #5 in exacta boxes. Understand, I'm not in self-destructive mode like Caan at the end of *The Gambler*, when he willingly puts himself in a position where he knows he'll be the victim of violence; I'm making these bets with the full expectation of seeing the #1 horse coming in first in race after race.

Shockingly, this highly scientific method results in a complete shutout. I drain the last of my Diet Coke and leave a $5 tip and about $600 in losing tickets on my table.

Back home, I check on the Citigroup stock I purchased for $2.81 a share at the outset of the adventure. A few days ago, it hit a high of $4.20 a share, but now it's down to $2.94, meaning it was basically a break-even "wager." (NOTE: in June 2009, Citigroup lost its coveted spot on the Dow Jones Industrial Average.)

As for other pending bets, it'll be months before the White Sox are mathematically eliminated from contention—even longer if they manage to make the playoffs. If they actually win the World Series, I'll get a payoff of $35,000 on my $1,000 bet. Realistically, I should put another $1,000 in the "loss" column—but for now I'm logging that bet as "open." I've also got a few hundred bucks still out there on wacky proposition bets—e.g., the fate of our beloved former governor Blago. Maybe I'll win that dream house in San Diego or one of the other prizes in the sweepstakes and raffles I entered. Not holding my breath on any of those. (NOTE: The Sox didn't come close to making the playoffs.)

I do win my "bet on the bet" with my friend Mel. As you'll recall, Mel issued a prop bet challenge saying I'd have a net loss of at least $15,000 over the 30-day period. If not for that Jim Thome homer in the White Sox game, I probably would have lost more than 15 grand overall—but with just a few hours left on the calendar, I'm in no danger of falling that low. So that's a $1,000 winner. Maybe I should have just made bets with Mel and Artie Lange all month.

Near midnight now. I've still got some action on a couple of West Coast games and a couple of horse races in Australia, but I've been eliminated from the last of the online poker tournaments I'd entered, and I've given up on the cash games after going card-dead for the last couple of hours.

Outside my office window, the muted sounds of the city play on. Cars and buses and the occasional motorcycle zipping past. Sirens. Patrons exiting Angels & Kings, their voices elevated after hours of drinking in a loud club.

In my office, the desktop, the two laptops, and the TV monitor are humming with activity. Scores, highlights, poker tournament results, live video from the last few remaining racetracks still running. The desk itself is covered with notes, receipts, lottery tickets, betting slips, etc. Little pieces of paper reminding me of financial risks of $50, $100, $300, $1,000 on various games of chance and skill.

Where has all this money gone? Well, I've helped out the governments of Illinois, Michigan, Indiana, Colorado, and a handful of other states with my lottery ticket purchases and my losses at various tracks and OTBs. I'd like to believe the cash I lost went directly into a fund designated for the purchase of a laptop for little Jimmy or Susie.

Whatever I lost on sports goes into Sid's pocket—or Sid has funneled it to someone who bet the other way. I have no problem with that. Sid provides a useful service—setting the lines and taking my action—and charges a 10 percent fee for that service. If I want to see Springsteen in concert, I have to pay a variety of service charges; so it goes with this particular form of entertainment.

The online poker losses go to other players, with the sites taking rake. As much as I hate losing, I'd rather lose at poker to a 22-year-old whiz kid in Amsterdam than drop thousands to Bodog.com at blackjack. Those are the losses that come the fastest and sting the hardest—me against the computerized robot dealer, getting shitty hand after shitty hand, stubbornly refusing to give up.

As the last couple of races and sporting events come to an end, I'm crunching the numbers and poring over my notes and records—and I feel as if I *just missed it*. If I had stayed away from all that online blackjack, if I'd played a little better and gotten a few more breaks in a couple of the tournaments, if I had been a little more careful with some of the bets on the ponies, I easily could be in the black right now. I know this wasn't supposed to be a how-to book on gambling—that the idea was to explore as many avenues as possible over the 30-day span . . . but still. I could have done that *and* come out a winner. Instead of feeling wiped out by the experience, oddly enough I'm energized, trying to figure out how I can get a rematch against the gambling gods.

The adventure is pretty much over. I haven't tallied up every single bet, but I'm down about $7,000, give or take a few hundred.

But in the immortal words of *Animal House*'s John Blutarsky, nothing is over until *we* decide it is. Early the next morning, I dash off an e-mail to Yuval Taylor, my trusty editor at Chicago Review Press, updating him on my progress and making a pitch: how about an epilogue? Yeah, that's it! An epilogue! There are a couple of big poker tournaments coming up in the next couple of weeks, and the Kentucky Derby is right around the corner. I should turn one of these events into a shot at redemption. In true gambler's fashion, what if I reached the end of the line—only to give myself an extension? (I'm like Gene Wilder in *Young Frankenstein*, who before entering the room containing the Monster says, "No matter what you hear in there . . . no matter how terribly I may scream, do not open this door . . ." and then ten seconds later is screaming, "Let me out of here! . . . What's the matter with you people? I was joking!") Wouldn't it be truly indicative of the gambler's personality if I gave myself a mulligan and made at least one last big bet *after* the 30 days were over?

Yuval's response: "Sounds good. I mean, it's not like you're going to give up gambling altogether after your 30 days' run, right? This book is a celebration of gambling, and if you're game to keep at it, that just shows you were right about it from the first."

Exactly! I love the thrill of the bet. I love the anticipation of the gamble. Yes, we dropped into some dark places over the last four weeks—and as long as we continue to risk money on these games, we know we will return to those dark places, again and again.

But the hunger lives. Even after making thousands of wagers totaling in the hundreds of thousands of dollars, the hunger lives. We can beat the odds. We can *win*.

I take a few days off from gambling in all forms. I sleep in, I eat right, I work out, I reconnect with friends, I read a book (*The Outliers*) that has nothing to do with gambling per se—though it does focus on probabilities and tendencies and the not-so-random nature of seemingly random occurrences.

As I organize the betting slips and the receipts and the lottery tickets and the notes for the book, I contemplate my options for the bonus round of betting.

Another poker tournament? There are a couple of big tourneys on the horizon, but the odds against a miraculous first-place finish or even a final table appearance are greatly stacked against me. What am I going to do, play for 11 hours, only to finish 37th out of 253 players?

I've already made a big bet on the White Sox. I could arrange an insane prop bet—find someone to wager $5,000 on the flip of a coin. Or I could walk into a casino and risk thousands on a single blackjack hand or the roll of a dice, and if I win I could double the bet, and if I win *again* I could double again. But even in the world of the risk-taker, that just seems too random and too reckless. If I started betting five grand on a single craps hand, then I'd be admitting my gambling has finally careened off the tracks.

The Kentucky Derby—that's the choice. The most exciting two minutes in all of sports could be the most profitable two minutes of my 2009 wagering season, if I back the right horse. I'll make reservations at the Stretch Run, I'll talk to some friends about making an afternoon/evening of it, I'll place one last big bet—and then I really, truly will call it a night on the great experiment. Whatever the bank-

roll is when they cross the finish line at Churchill Downs, that's where the bankroll will stay.

By the time I drift off to sleep on the Tuesday night before the Derby, I have already decided I'll be betting big on the race—but I've yet to make a selection. All I know is, I'm not going to bet on the favorite.

Somewhere deep in the night, it begins to rain. The dream hits you at three o'clock in the morning . . .

Epilogue

Bankroll:
−$7,000

"The 4 horse! Nobody bets the 4 horse, Trotter. The 4 horse is a joke.
They let little kiddies on the 4 horse to have their picture taken."
—From the 1989 movie *Let it Ride*

As post time approaches, the buzz in the Stretch Run grows louder.
Every track in the country takes a break during the Derby, so
every monitor in the joint is tuned to the telecast, as the 19 horses are
in the gate and ready to go.

"And they're off in the Kentucky Derby!" calls Tom Durkin, the
thoroughbred announcer for NBC. "And it's Join in the Dance who's
racing for the lead, Musket Man has some early speed on the inside,
Regal Ransom with some speed as well, beneath the twin spires for
the first time . . ."

Less than two minutes later, they're around the turn and heading
for home, with Join in the Dance and Pioneer of the Nile and Regal
Ransom battling for first . . .

"As the field turns for home, top of the stretch, it's still Join in the
Dance with a tenuous lead," says Durkin. "Regal Ransom and Pioneer

of the Nile strike the front . . . Musket Man is coming hard . . . and Papa Clem's right there . . ."

And then something amazing happens—something that catches even Durkin by surprise. He's still calling the names of the aforementioned three horses when a long shot comes blazing out of nowhere on the rail, blowing by everyone else in the stretch. Durkin actually stops himself as he tries to figure out which horse is in the process of shocking the world, and by the time he calls this horse's name, the race is essentially over and he can't suppress a chuckle as we all bear witness to perhaps the greatest upset in the history of the Kentucky Derby.

"Coming on through, that is, uh, Mine That Bird, now's coming on to take the lead . . . and in a spectacular, spectacular upset, Mine That Bird has won the Kentucky Derby, an impossible result here!"

In the Stretch Run in Chicago, the huge crowd is nearly silent. Who the hell is Mine That Bird? What was his number again? Did anyone have this 50-1 long shot? Anyone at all?

(Ron Magers, a popular veteran anchorman in Chicago and a longtime breeder and owner of thoroughbreds, told me a story about an esteemed horseman he knows who saw Mine That Bird on an exercise run a few weeks before the race. The man had said, "Well, at least he won't get in the way of the good horses.")

Mine That Bird's number is 8.

Deep breath. Exhale.

Alas, that is not the number I saw dancing in front of me on the night of the dream. The number I saw was 3. The horse I bet on was Mr. Hot Stuff, who went off at 28-1 and never threatened. As far as I know, Mr. Hot Stuff is still trying to make it around the oval at Churchill Downs.

The winning horse went off at 50-1. Mine That Bird paid $103.20 for a $2 bet. Had I taken Mine That Bird, I would have won more than $40,000. Had I placed Mine That Bird in an exacta box with Pioneer of the Nile, I would have won at least another $20,000.

But that's what everyone is saying, right? *Woulda, coulda, shoulda.*

At my table, we all lament the end of the dream—the dream I had earlier in the week, and the dream I had of turning the epilogue of this book into a storybook ending.

I glance at the program, checking out the chart on one of the biggest upset winners in the history of horse racing. Might as well find out a little bit about this horse called Mine That Bird.

And there it is, in stark black and white.

Mine That Bird was sired by Birdstone.

Birdstone. The horse that scored what may have been the biggest surprise of the decade—at least until today's race.

Birdstone. The horse in the framed photo hanging in my sports room. The horse that gave me the biggest single wagering victory of my life in 2004 when he shocked the world by passing Smarty Jones in the stretch at the Belmont.

Birdstone! Mine That Bird! How could I possibly have missed that?

My phone lights up with a text message from a friend who was with me in 2004 for that Birdstone triumph. "I know you had that!" he writes. "How much did you win?"

Uh . . .

I share the story of Birdstone with my tablemates. They're sympathetic, but they can't believe I didn't bet on Mine That Bird because of a dream on some other horse. Mine That Bird was a horse of destiny! I can rationalize it a thousand ways to Sunday, but the truth is they're right. If not for the dream, I would have gone through my normal ritual of reading up on all the entrants in the Derby, looking for a sign. Birdstone is the sire of Mine That Bird? Yeah, that would have qualified as a sign. But because of the dream about that #3 horse winning, because I locked myself into the dream, because I didn't dare go against the dream out of fear the damn horse would win and I'd be kicking myself forever, I didn't even bother to study up on the race. I had my selections and I had 'em in stone. There was no point in looking any further.

The crowd at the Stretch Run begins to thin out, although some stick around for the upcoming Bulls-Celtics playoff game. (I have

no money on the basketball game. I'm off the sports bets. I probably won't make another wager on a game until the Super Bowl of next year, and I won't miss it for a second.) My group is ready to move on, but I suggest we have another round of drinks and bet just one more race. I can't let Mine That Bird have the last word.

It's five minutes to post at Arlington Park, and I convince everyone to join me in a wager on the #1 horse, True Brew. Even though I don't believe in being "due," even though I realize there is absolutely no connection between my failure to bet on Mine That Bird and the next bet I make, even though I know better than to believe in hunches or streaks, I'm going to bet this damn horse and it's going to win, and then we're going to walk out of here and I won't look back.

True Brew goes off at 5-2, but as the horses near the half-mile mark he trails the field. Whatever. Another few hundred bucks ain't gonna make a difference anyway.

And then he makes a move on the rail, just like Mine That Bird made a move on the rail in the Derby less than a half hour ago. It might be too late for him to overtake every horse in front of him, but he's got a shot at second—not that I have any money on him to finish second or third. As usual, it's all or nothing.

It appears a horse named Here We Go Again is going to take it. *Here We Go Again.* Is somebody trying to tell me something?

"And True Brew comes up the fence," cries the announcer. "They're homeward bound . . . Here We Go Again . . . True Brew with a late gain, True Brew getting up to win it from Here We Go Again!"

Winner. We've got a winner. It's about 1 percent of what I would have netted had I bet on Mine That Bird in the Derby, but have I really reached the point where I can't enjoy a $780 profit on a single race?

Normally I'd say no, but even as I cash the winning ticket and stuff the hundreds into my money clip, I'm cursing under my breath about that goddamn dream that died a quick death but kept me away from the horse I *should* have been betting.

It's time for a break. Even if I hadn't planned on the Derby being the final step of the journey, it would have been time for a break.

When you're steaming about a lost opportunity to win $60,000 or more, when you know it was your *destiny* to win that 60 grand but you neglected to answer the door when destiny came a-knockin', you need some time to distance yourself from the disappointment and get your mind right.

Breathe in. Breathe out.

Bankroll:
−$7,500

Like just about anyone who has spent big chunks of time risking money on games of chance and skill, I've had those moments where I've thought about trying to do it full time. I'd think: I could take six months or a year off and hit the poker circuit, with side "jobs" playing blackjack and betting on sports. (The horses? Not so much.) Rent a house in Vegas, travel to the big tournaments, turn the 30-year hobby into a full-time gig.

Now, after 30 straight days of gambling (plus bonus time)—now I know I'd never want to do that. I'm not going to make some empty proclamation about never gambling again, because I know I'll be playing poker before the month is out and I'll probably be in Vegas again before the year is done—but I am certain I don't want to dedicate myself full time to the thrill of the risk, with all its temporary highs and ulcer-inducing lows. If I'd spent as much time learning a foreign language or studying the guitar as I have gambling, I'd be fluent in French or I'd have mastered "Layla" by now. (Yes, even when I engage in speculation, it's of the selfish variety.) If I woke up every morning knowing I'd be spending the day (and maybe the night) gambling, I could see myself spiraling downward, into ever-darker places. Maybe I'd never become as self-destructive as James Caan in *The Gambler*— but I couldn't guarantee that wouldn't happen.

Would I ever do another 30-day experiment? Maybe—but if I did it again, I'd want to see how I'd do playing only the games I'd normally play. For the purposes of the book, I wanted to include as many gambling opportunities as I could gobble up in a month. Hence the sweepstakes entries, the lottery ticket, the visit to the dog track, the dozens of relatively uninformed bets on horse races at tracks I'd never heard of. Those were almost guaranteed built-in losses. What if I played only poker and blackjack, and bet only on teams I really followed? Could I do that for a month and wind up in the black? I'd like to think so. I might just have to find out.

What did I learn from this experience? Are you kidding me? Who said anything about learning anything? I didn't learn a damn thing. I already knew baccarat is a sucker's game, the lottery is a mirage for 99.9 percent of players, the slots are nearly impossible to beat, and if you're risking good money on dogs chasing after a mechanical rabbit, you deserve to lose. On the plus side, I've long been in favor of playing the Pass Line and taking the odds in craps, making smart, by-the-book plays in blackjack, and taking the occasional leap of faith on a hoops game. I was just trying to get *you* to see the light, my friend. But let's face it—if you're the kind of gambler who believes certain numbers are "due" in roulette, if you love playing the Wheel of Fortune slots, if you buy $50 worth of lottery tickets every week, if you think you have a super-system for winning at blackjack—you're not going to change your routine. And if you're a nongambler, I'm sure you've been horrified at some of the stories I told. Here's hoping you were amused to an equal degree.

As I walk into the late afternoon with my friends, laughing and talking and, yes, still lamenting the bets not made on the Derby, I'm reminded once again of the ridiculously corny but nonetheless undeniable truth about my life and how blessed I've been, with such a wonderful family, so many great and lasting friends, such incredible professional fortune. I don't need to gamble all the time. I won the life lottery, and it's not because I deserved it more than anyone else.

Turns out I believe in blind luck after all.

After its stunning upset victory as a 50-1 long shot in the Kentucky Derby and a strong second-place finish in the Preakness, Mine That Bird was the favorite to win the Belmont Stakes. And, indeed, Mine That Bird was in the lead as they headed for home—but he ran out of gas down the stretch and finished third.

The winner? An unheralded three-year-old named Summer Bird, at 11-1.

Like Mine That Bird, Summer Bird was sired by Birdstone.

At post time for the Belmont, the author had the White Sox–Indians game playing on the TV in his office as he put the finishing touches on this book. He did not learn of the Belmont Stakes results until he started receiving texts from friends asking if he had gone with the other Birdstone connection this time around.

The answer is no.

Index